W9-ABK-665

Toward the Flame

A MEMOIR OF WORLD WAR I

By HERVEY ALLEN

Illustrated by Lyle Justis

INTRODUCTION TO THE BISON BOOKS EDITION BY
Steven Trout

UNIVERSITY OF NEBRASKA PRESS • LINCOLN AND LONDON

Copyright © 1926, 1934 by Hervey Allen
Introduction © 2003 by the University of Nebraska Press
All rights reserved
Manufactured in the United States of America

⊗

First Nebraska paperback printing: 2003

Library of Congress Cataloging-in-Publication Data
Allen, Hervey, 1889–1949.
Toward the flame : a memoir of World War I / by Hervey Allen ;
illustrated by Lyle Justis ; introduction by Steven Trout.
p.   cm.
Originally published: New York : Farrar & Rinehart, 1926.
ISBN 0-8032-5947-6 (pbk. : alk. paper)
1. Allen, Hervey, 1889–1949.   2. World War, 1914–1918—Personal
narratives, American.   3. World War, 1914–1918—Campaigns—
Western Front.   I. Title.
D570.9.A53   2003
940.4'1273'092—dc21
[B]   2002075091

STEVEN TROUT

Introduction

First published in 1926, Hervey Allen's *Toward the Flame* is that rarest of war memoirs—a deeply moving account that both resists easy classification (the reader is allowed to decide whether the narrative offers a tribute to American soldiery or a call for pacifism) and displays fresh nuances upon each rereading. Depicting a mere six weeks during the summer of 1918, the book tells an elegantly simple story. The story opens with Lieutenant Allen's company of Pennsylvania National Guardsmen marching inland from the French coast, amid sunshine and subdued greetings from civilians, and then follows the unit's descent into the fierce and unpredictable open warfare that characterized the Second Battle of the Marne. The narrative ends abruptly after documenting the disastrous fighting at the village of Fismette, where Allen was seriously wounded and his band of fellow Pennsylvanians nearly wiped out—all due to the misjudgment and callousness of one French general.

Allen jettisons all the predictable elements found in standard narratives about World War I: there is no rendering of stateside training or the voyage to France, no account of how the commander (the narrator) came to "bond" with his men, and no expression of regimental or divisional esprit de corps; at the same time there is no indication of the sense of brotherhood that soldiers in the First World War supposedly felt toward their adversaries. (Of the enemy, Allen writes, "I disliked the Germans, but I disliked them because I feared them, knowing full well their deadly capability" [140].) In place of those familiar formulas *Toward the Flame* offers a succession of scenes and images, photographic in their intensity and detail, that capture the essence of combat during the final summer of the conflict. The book is, above all else, the work of an intelligent observer whose camera-like gaze misses nothing. In his preface to the 1934 illustrated edition, Allen stressed that he had attempted to avoid relating "a personal adventure." He had sought, he explained, "to eliminate the big 'I' of little ego and to substitute for it only the first person singular of the fellow who happened, under certain circumstances, to be around" (xxii). To a remarkable degree Allen succeeded in achieving this objective, even going so far as to omit any details regarding his severe wounding at Fismette and subsequent recovery. Allen could not, however, prevent certain features of his quietly attractive personality from dominating the narrative—especially his insatiable curiosity, a quality that paradoxically serves the narrative's appearance of impersonal reportage.

Throughout the book Allen *has* to know. Indeed, his curiosity even leads him into the ever-shifting no man's land between the German and American forces. At one point, for example, we watch as Allen reconnoiters in advance of his own army, creeping fearfully—yet with a strange sense of exhilaration—through deceptively peaceful forests and fields, sometimes narrowly avoiding bands of Germans. The author's compulsion to witness the topsy-turvy world of war in all its complexities manifests itself just as memorably in scenes set on the edge of the killing zone. With an almost archaeological thoroughness Allen sifts through the rubble of a demolished French village, taking note of each poignant artifact. Ever mindful of possible booby traps, he explores captured German dugouts, sinister yet alluring places strewn with alien-looking military equipment. And, in a scene whose panoramic vistas stand in stark contrast to the often claustrophobic world of the front line's foxholes and underground command posts, he journeys some miles westward to observe the buildup of American troops and war materiel in forests and towns only recently seized from the Germans. With characteristic attention to the perceptual subtleties of a war experience, Allen remarks, "All the intensity and mystery that the presence of the enemy lends to a place had gone" (175). From beginning to end Allen is a restless traveler, ever anxious to see what is happening to the sides, front, and rear of his own unit. He is the perfect window into war.

So, who was this remarkable observer, this perfect window? Born into a prominent Pittsburgh family in 1889, William Hervey Allen Jr. entered the U.S. Naval Academy in 1909, only to suffer an athletic injury two years later that forced him to drop out. In 1915 he graduated from the University of Pittsburgh with a bachelor's degree in economics (Allen's alma mater today houses his papers), and in 1916 he served on the Mexican border as a member of the 18th Pennsylvania Infantry, a Pittsburgh-based National Guard regiment. Camp life in Texas, spent on the lookout for invading revolutionaries who never materialized, gave Allen enough free time to pen his first book, a collection of Kipling-esque verse titled *Ballads of the Border.*

In the summer of 1917 the 18th Pennsylvania merged with another local National Guard unit to form the 111th Infantry Regiment, part of the 28th Division of the American Expeditionary Forces (AEF). Fresh from his tame adventures in the American Southwest, Allen prepared to experience a real war. A souvenir booklet created several months before Allen's regiment left for Europe, titled *A Short History and Illustrated Roster of the 111th Infantry,* captures the pride, innocence, and gung-ho spirit of the weekend warriors with whom he served.[1] The "short history" emphasizes the decades of martial tradition that stood behind the 111th Infantry—despite the organization's freshly created, generic title—by offering an inspiring retrospective of Pittsburgh's contribution to earlier national emergencies, from the Mexican-American War of 1848 through the recent border mobilization. The "illustrated roster" concludes with a photograph of each canine member of the regiment (one per company). Like their human comrades, "Kaiser," "Bum," "Shepp," and other assorted collies and retrievers look confidently into the camera, as if eager to embark upon the Great Adventure.

Presumably with mascots in tow, the 111th Infantry traveled from Pittsburgh to Camp Hancock, Georgia, in late 1917; after several months of training it embarked for Europe aboard the HMS *Olympic*, the sister ship (as many of the doughboys jovially noted) of the *Titanic*. In order to minimize exposure to German submarines the regiment landed first in Britain, then crossed the English Channel from Southampton to St. Nazaire, France, on 14 May 1918. After an interval of further training—first with the British, and then with the French—the 111th moved into the Marne sector in early July.

As it turned out, Allen arrived on the Western Front at a critical moment. With a huge influx of fresh manpower created by the Russian withdrawal from the war in 1917, the German Army had weakened British and French defenses in the spring of 1918 and, through a series of effective attacks, had pushed the front line alarmingly close to Paris. By early June, however, this all-out bid to win the war (before the United States could effectively train and transport its millions of draft-eligible men) had begun to bog down. During the Third Battle of the Aisne River (27 May–2 June) German forces fell short of their objectives—partly due to the surprising tenacity displayed by American troops at Château-Thierry and Belleau Wood. A subsequent German attack, the Noyon-Montdidier Offensive (9–13 June), also failed to produce a decisive victory.

On 15 July, as Allen and his comrades acclimated themselves to life at the front, the Germans launched their final and most disastrous offensive, a massive feint intended to carry the war still closer to Paris and thus draw Allied reserves from Flanders, where the German High Command hoped to achieve a war-winning breakthrough. Known as the Second Battle of the Marne, the ensuing bloodbath (in which the Germans alone suffered nearly two hundred thousand casualties) began successfully for the attackers with the creation of a twenty-two-mile-wide salient in the Allied line and the establishment of a bridgehead on the southern bank of the Marne River. However, French and American resistance prevented the Germans from widening their position, and by early August Allied counterattacks had not only crushed the Germans' bridgehead but had recaptured most of the territory in the Aisne-Marne region occupied by the enemy since May. What began as a diversionary stab toward Paris ended with the Kaiser's Army on the defensive and any plans for a final "peace offensive" permanently shelved.

As vividly depicted in *Toward the Flame*, the 111th Infantry was thrown into the middle of this colossal battle and received its torturous initiation into combat while advancing on foot (often in a sleep-deprived stupor) all the way from the Marne to the Vesle River. The fighting Allen and his men experienced bore little resemblance to familiar World War I images of trenches and charges across no man's land. Instead, the Second Battle of the Marne offered its participants all the terrors and satisfactions of so-called open warfare, as the rigid lines of fortification ordinarily associated with the Western Front collapsed into an amorphous jumble of friend and foe virtually impenetrable to the military intelligence of the day. Like the GIs of the Second World War, Allen and his men advanced across a beautiful but treacherous landscape, often uncertain if the next village or cluster of trees contained American troops or German machine gunners.

Ironically, the 111th Infantry faced its severest trial in the days that immediately followed the official close of the Second Battle of the Marne. By 5 August the regiment had helped push the Germans to a new defensive line located more than twenty miles north of Château-Thierry. Yet Maj. Gen. Jean Degoutte, the French Army commander under whom the 28th Division served, wanted more. Working from faulty intelligence—and even faultier military doctrine—Degoutte ordered the capture of Fismette, a village located on the German-controlled north bank of the Vesle and accessible only by a half-demolished bridge continually being swept by machine-gun bullets and shell fragments.[2] Somehow several companies from the 112th Infantry, the sister regiment of the 111th, managed to occupy the town. By the time Allen led his men across the bridge several days later, however, it was obvious to everyone except Degoutte that the position was untenable. Enemy snipers still occupied many of the buildings, and German artillery and machine-gun fire poured onto the Americans from the surrounding hillsides. A helpless witness to the death or wounding of most of his companions, Allen lasted in this ruinous inferno (which finally fell to the Germans on 28 August) for four days—until wounds inflicted by mustard gas and high explosives necessitated his removal to a French base hospital. He had lived, just barely, through one of the most notorious blunders of 1918, a clear example of coalition war-making at its worst.

The nightmarish house-to-house fighting at Fismette provides the climactic finale to Allen's memoir. It is the terrible flame toward which the book's escalating horrors inexorably lead. However, Allen's overseas service did not end there. After recovering from his wounds he rejoined what was left of his unit for the Meuse-Argonne Offensive, where the AEF operated as an autonomous army (in part because of incidents like Fismette); Allen then finished out his overseas service by working as a translator with the French Army.

As evidenced by his correspondence, Allen felt an immediate impulse to write of what he had seen, especially the hellish scenes at Fismette. In lengthy letters to family and friends he recounted his experiences and, in 1919, collected his personal impressions of the Second Battle of the Marne into a narrative tentatively titled "In the Wake of the Ebb."[3] Perhaps sensing that he required more time to digest his still-painful ordeal, Allen put the manuscript aside. He spent most of the 1920s in a series of teaching positions (including lectureships at Columbia University and Vassar College) and focused much of his creative effort on poetry, publishing his second collection of verse, *Wampum and Old Gold*, in 1921. One of the poems in the collection, a war ballad titled "The Blindman," eventually appeared as a separate volume, and helped establish its author's reputation as a sensitive and literate witness to war.

Accomplished as Allen was as a poet (in all he produced six volumes of poetry and drew praise for his verse from numerous critics), two important publications, both released in 1926, revealed

prose as his true forte. The first was *Israfel*, a major biography of
Edgar Allen Poe; the second, *Toward the Flame*, a disciplined re-
working of "In the Wake of the Ebb." Reviewers responded warmly
to both works—especially the latter. For example, in his notice for
The Bookman, John Farrar (later Allen's publisher) described *Toward the Flame* as "unforgettable and beautiful. It has the marks of a
classic, and will be read as long as the World War is remembered"
(223).[4] Similarly, Lawrence S. Morris of *The New Republic* proclaimed,
"None of the official or unofficial war records yet published sur-
passes the detached, authentic ring of this personal account." Like
many reviewers Morris highlighted the absence of an explicit
agenda in Allen's narrative: "Every reader may draw his own moral.
It has been easy to see gods, villains, and clowns inside of uniforms. Mr. Allen saw human beings" (147).[5]

Allen's neutral tone served the book well at a time when the
personal literature of the First World War had become largely po-
larized. The best-known American war novels from the period—
such as John Dos Passos's *Three Soldiers* (1921), Thomas Boyd's
Through the Wheat (1923), Laurence Stallings's *Plumes* (1924), and
William Faulkner's *Soldier's Pay* (1926)—all mocked, in one way or
another, the abstract ideals for which the "Great War for Civilization" had been fought. Filled with bitterly ironic scenes of deprav-
ity and horror, such works expressed a profound sense of disillu-
sionment. However, the vast majority of American war memoirs
published between 1919 and 1929, volumes far less familiar to
readers today, upheld the opposite view—that American interven-
tion in the Great War had in fact constituted a noble crusade.[6]
Unwilling to focus solely on battlefield misery and carnage and, at
the same time, indifferent to conventional patriotism, Allen's narrative falls into neither camp. In his climactic portrayal of the
debacle at Fismette, Allen acknowledges the stupidity and callousness that often reigned supreme within the Allied war effort.
However, *Toward the Flame* also includes countless instances of courage, compassion, and fortitude. War, the book shows us, is a com-
plex activity that draws upon every human emotion and capacity,
both noble and savage.

Allen's refusal to simplify what he had experienced during the summer of 1918 impressed enough reviewers and readers to keep *Toward the Flame* in print throughout the late 1920s and early 1930s. The 1934 illustrated edition, reproduced here, owes its existence, at least in part, to circumstances unrelated to the narrative's merits. One year earlier, Hervey Allen became a household name through the success of his novel *Anthony Adverse*, a 1,224-page epic set during the Napoleonic era. One of the best-selling historical novels of the twentieth century, the book captured an international audience, inspired a successful Hollywood adaptation (starring Fredric March and Olivia de Havilland), and ultimately made its author a wealthy man. Farrar & Rinehart's decision to reissue *Toward the Flame* in a larger, more elegant format, complete with Lyle Justis's evocative drawings, probably had as much to do with Allen's sudden name recognition and marketability as it did with the respectable following that the original edition, published by George Doran, had inspired among World War I veterans.

For the rest of his life, which a heart attack suddenly ended in 1949, Allen focused his career primarily on historical fiction, producing such noteworthy examples of the genre as *Action at Aquila* (1938), set during the American Civil War, and *The Forest and the Fort* (1943), part of a five-volume series that focused on pre-Revolutionary War Pennsylvania and remained unfinished at the writer's death. Indeed, it is primarily as a historical novelist that Allen is remembered today. However, *Toward the Flame* may yet prove to be his most important work. In his preface to *It Was Like This*, a pair of First World War stories published on the eve of America's entry into the Second World War, Allen wrote, "Human habits change slowly, and war is, perhaps, the oldest mass habit of all" (13). One of the finest narratives ever to record the contradictory emotions and behaviors produced by the "mass habit" of war, *Toward the Flame* never preaches, simplifies, or resorts to familiar conventions. By acknowledging both the fascinations and the repellant horrors of battle, the book provides a unique portrait of World War I—and of our deepest selves.

NOTES

My thanks to Richard F. Allen for his willingness to verify the biographical details contained here. I am also indebted to Charlie Aston and Malkiel Choseed of the University of Pittsburgh for making available various materials contained in the Hervey Allen Collection.

1. *A Short History and Illustrated Roster of the 111th Infantry, United States* (Philadelphia: Edward Stern, 1918).

2. For a historical account of the fighting at Fismette see John Kennedy Ohl, "The Keystone Division in the Great War" *Prologue* (summer 1978): 83–99. Ohl attributes Degoutte's murderous orders to a combination of French military doctrine, which held that advancing troops should always establish bridgeheads (regardless of the strength of the enemy), and Degoutte's own personal motives: "Rumors abounded that the French high command planned to break up the Sixth Army to replace losses in other armies, and Degoutte feared that he would be reduced to a corps commander in this consolidation if he deviated from the high command's directive" (97).

3. This manuscript is contained in the Hervey Allen Collection at the Hillman Library of the University of Pittsburgh.

4. John Farrar review of *Toward the Flame* in *The Bookman* 63.2 (April 1926): 222–23.

5. Lawrence S. Morris, "Flame and Ash," review of *Toward the Flame* in *The New Republic* 47.603 (23 June 1926): 147–48.

6. See, for example, Carl E. Haterius's *Reminiscences of the 137th U.S. Infantry* (Topeka: Crane, 1919); Frank Holden's *War Memories* (Athens GA: Athens Book, 1922); and Elmer W. Sherwood's *The Diary of a Rainbow Veteran* (Terre Haute: Moore-Langen, 1929).

TO SIDNEY HOWARD

PREFACE

I HAVE tried to reproduce in words my experience in France during the great war. There is no plot, no climax, no happy ending to this book. It is a narrative, plain, unvarnished, without heroics, and true. It is what I saw as nearly as memory has preserved it, and I have set it down as a picture of war with no comment, except a very little here and there by way of explanation. This book shows how it looked "over there."

The narrative covers the drive from the Marne to the Vesle during the fateful months of July and August, 1918, from about July first to August fourteenth. It gives a glimpse of some of the fighting about Château-Thierry and Fismes, but above all, it shows how we lived and died, ate, cooked, looked, thought and felt during that time. It is the intimate detail of life at the front as I saw it, and pretends to

Preface

be nothing more. As a personal narrative told in the first person it is only natural that I appear in it myself.

About half of this material was written in a long letter from a hospital in France immediately after the events which it relates. The rest was set down in 1919 just after my return to the United States when the memories were still so strong as to be almost photographic.

In reading over this account again six years after the war, I find that I was mistaken at times as to the reasons for certain troop movements and disciplinary measures, and in one or two instances even as to my exact whereabouts on a given date. But I have not changed the text in the light of after knowledge, as the preservation of the exact state of mind and even of the prejudices of the times and place are part of the book's essential verity and have perhaps a minor value in themselves. In *some places,* for obvious reasons, personal names have been slightly changed and some military terms and objects have been spoken of in everyday language.

It is a purely personal narrative. Those who look for a discussion of military policies or tactics will be disappointed. This book is not propaganda of any kind. It is much more than that; it is a picture of war, broken off when the film burned out.

HERVEY ALLEN.

New York,
December, 1925.

PREFACE TO THIS EDITION

SINCE *Toward the Flame* was first published in the spring of 1926 there have been several editions, including a number of reprints.

In a very quiet manner, unchampioned, unaccompanied by anything but the best critical comment—that of one reader to another—the book has gradually taken its place as one of those volumes by an American about the World War, which for one reason or another continues to be widely read. So gradual was the process, however, that the author himself would not have been aware of it had it not been for a constant trickle of letters from readers all over the country. Nevertheless, over thirty thousand copies have now been sold, the last reprint is exhausted, and another is called for. The publishers have therefore taken the opportunity of providing a new format for the volume, which, it is hoped, will be found for several reasons to be more attractive than the old.

In particular it is thought that the illustrations of Mr. Lyle Justis will not only help to bring home to the reader the reality of the scenes here described, but what is more difficult, serve to make evident the general spirit animating those Americans who participated in the great Allied offensive of the summer of 1918.

Preface to This Edition

The artist himself took part as a soldier in the events he depicts. He knows his types, his locale, and his atmosphere. His illustrations are therefore the result of imagination drawing upon genuine personal experience.

So rapidly have the details and peculiar aspects of the scenes of the Great War tended to fall into oblivion that it seems essential to point out at this writing that *Toward the Flame* is not a story about professional soldiers glorifying the exploits of some particular unit. It is merely that of one of many of the National Guard units of the American army. But as such, *it is that cross section of the citizens in arms, and actually engaged in battle, which the narrator observed and did his best to report.*

In the preface to earlier editions, which is here included, and which I wish new readers would read, I refer to the fact that "This story ends where the film burns out." That is quite literally true.

It was not the object of this book merely to relate a personal adventure. I tried, insofar as anyone can, to eliminate the big "I" of little ego and to substitute for it only the first person singular of the fellow who happened, under certain circumstances, to be around. Hence, I ended the story with the night attack on the village of Fismette, when most of the defenders of that place had ceased to exist. If I did not inflict upon my readers certain personal sufferings and physical indignities that followed, it was because I felt that they were important to me alone. In other words, I meant this to be a report of what I saw on the battle line, and when the fighting ends the story stops.

In answer, however, to many letters and innumerable questions as to what *did* happen to me, I can now, after sixteen years, "hasten to add" that in the early morning hours after the attack, and in the company of one sergeant, I managed to return to headquarters where I was promptly tagged by our regimental surgeon and sent to a base hospital.

To him, and to that surgeon, whoever he was, who in a certain field hospital saved my eyes from the effect of mustard gas and tended other injuries, I should like at this time to express what the word "gratitude" only too coldly conveys. But that is another story.

And since the story of behind the lines is essentially different from the story of the battlefront this book has nothing to do with the former.

A more general and official view of the fighting about Fismes and Fismette, and of the events described in the last chapters of this volume will be found in the correspondence of some of the generals in charge of the operations, which are included as addenda at the back of the book.

These pages were originally rather hastily prepared for the press, after they had lain about in manuscript for some years. Indeed, they were not meant to be a book at all. Most of the material was taken from letters I had written home from the front or from the hospital, describing experiences on the battle line, and from notes jotted in a rough diary—all of which were very casual, and, I am afraid, rather incoherent.

After returning home in 1919, I found myself much troubled at night by memories of the war and often unable to sleep. It occurred to me then that I might rid myself of my subjective war by trying to make it objective in writing. Taking in hand the material mentioned above, and adding to it what I still so vividly remembered, I whipped the whole into shape without any thought at the time of publishing it. The medicine worked, although perhaps the style of the utterance suffered.

In preparing this edition for the press, however, I have reread proofs, altered the sentence structure here and there, removed some obscurities, and clarified the punctuation. But remembering that the book as a whole was set down at white heat with the full vividness of the scene unbearably in mind, I have let the text stand substantially unaltered.

H. A.

December, 1933.

CONTENTS

Toward the Flame

CHAPTER I

ROUTE MARCHING

C AN ANY one who took part in those route
marches in France from the sea to the front
ever forget them? It seems to me that we were always marching along those splendid, shaded, French
roads with a gridiron of sunshine falling through the
tree trunks that stretched their endless, double row
along the white ribbon that disappeared forever and

3

forever over the edge of the next hill. Here, there was a bright space and a row of stumps where the necessities of war had cut down the precious shade of the highway, and then, we were entering a long vista where the branches met in a Gothic arch overhead.

It was like a river flowing through a tunnel, a river of men.

There is a glimpse of the major and his adjutant on horses ahead; blotches of sunshine on the brown khaki, like spots of paint on an autumn leaf; a tangle of rifles at all angles and positions; the sweating neck of the man in front of you, and the ceaseless swing of legs like the drivers of some gigantic engine.

That was the way it looked in the summer before we had much rain.

Then there were ten-minute halts, just long enough for you to get stiff, but welcome nevertheless. And what a throwing away of cigarette butts when the word came to *fall in!* Then another plod of twenty minutes, with that pack-strap and belt giving you a toothache in the back, till the single long blast of the bugle called the next halt and the brown squares of men disappeared off the white road like magic—always to the right—so the important little side cars and the colonels' automobiles could dash up and down.

So it went many and many a time.

The route from St. Denis-Rebais to Petit Villiers,

which was to be our next halting place, lay through the town of Rebais, twisting around through the narrow streets in a confusing fashion so that our connecting files had a busy time of it. It is no light thing to turn a wrong corner when a whole division is following you. Explanations might, to say the least, be impracticable, so I was very glad to see the figure of our connecting file at each corner and hear a well-known voice say, "This way, lieutenant,"— then *column right* or *left*—and there was the rear of "A" company with the smoking cooker just disappearing around the next corner of the street.

Toward the Flame

The whole population turned out to see us. Women held up their babies to *Les braves Américains* as we went by down the streets between the shuttered stone houses. We remarked the absence of any cheap cries or "home town" cheers; only a tense exclamation once in a while, or the fierce exhortation of some wounded *poilu*. For the most part there was complete silence, except for the everlasting ring of steel boot-nails on hard stones.

There was a sameness, a uniformity, about our army that was new to the French, used to so many different styles of uniforms; a Saxon vigor and sternness, too, which for all their dash and gallantry, our Latin allies lacked. This was a bigger race of men passing, company after company, regiment after regiment, brigade and division.

Rebais was not a very large town so it was not long before we were out of its streets, and marching up and down the light rises of the low, undulating, cultivated country that lay beyond. Here for the first time we became conscious that we were really near the front. Miles away against the skyline hung a captive balloon; the whole air was constantly vibrating like a sympathetic bell with the whirring sound of planes, too high to be visible; and suddenly there was the far-off powder-puff burst of anti-aircraft shells about the "sausage," followed a long while later by faint double reports. They were the first we had seen and heard. "So that was the front up there!" Men looked at each other significantly.

Presently the road zigzagged down into a steep valley with a stream, a bridge, and an empty, gaping town at the bottom, where we made a halt. The mess sergeant brought me the unpleasant news that the fire had gone out in our senile rolling kitchen; the old grates couldn't stand the jolting of the road. But since I knew this meant that the faithful kitchen detail must have put up a brave but losing fight, I could not have much to say except to join in with a few hearty blessings on its former hapless owners, H. M. Royal Scots.

Nevertheless, the news was unwelcome. The men expected to be fed, and they looked to the officers to feed them. To feed, clothe, equip, and pay the men,—that is about all a line officer can do anyway,—pictures of sword flourishers in battle notwithstanding. Excuses make cold fare, and I had visions of our outfit sitting alongside the road while "A" company and "C" company fed full. A look into the boilers, however, with pieces of half-raw meat and potatoes floating in the lukewarm water, convinced me that nothing could be done, for just about that time we were on the move again. Such little things as this are what make the soldier's life "so romantic," housekeeping on the flowing road with 250 ravenous children.

The deserted town we passed through looked very

7

desolate and lonely. It was the first place we had seen which the inhabitants had abandoned, and it gave one much the same sensation as passing through a cemetery at night. The village had not been shelled, but the balance was being held so precariously at Château-Thierry just then that a good many of the villages were being deserted. Any day the line might swing one way or the other. Here the inhabitants had left.

We toiled up the steep road toward the plateau on the other side of the valley, and finally made a halt near the top, where the subject of lunch once more became acute. The men began to look suspiciously at our "fireless" cooker, and I began to contemplate making a dicker for some hot coffee with Captain Williams of "A" company, when something occurred which drove all ideas of eating completely out of our minds.

There were no iron rations used on the sly that day!

"The colonel desires to see you and Lieutenant Shenkel, sir," said the colonel's chauffeur as he drove up in the commanding officer's car. "Jump in." I knew the "old man" must want to see us pretty badly if he sent his car, and as we whirled up the road, I anxiously passed in review my conduct of the last few days, which I am bound to say had been that of an officer and a gentleman. I glanced at Shenkel, who looked as innocent as ever. Well, we should soon know—here was the colonel now.

He was standing by the roadside with the adjutant and Captain Law,* where they had been having a hurried bite to eat, and he looked at us rather gravely as we came up and saluted him.

"The French general commanding at Château-Thierry has asked for two platoons from the 28th Division to coöperate with the French in an attack which is to take place to-night at Hill 204," said the colonel. "I have sent for you because we want this regiment to participate, and I am going to send one platoon from 'A' company under Lieutenant Bentz and one from 'B' company under you, Lieutenant Shenkel. You and the company commander can decide what platoon it is to be. We cannot conveniently get in touch with the other battalions now, there is no time to lose, so both platoons will go from this battalion."

We both saluted and fairly ran down the road back to the company. Of course, Shenkel would take his own platoon, the

---

* This officer, the captain of the author's company, was at this time acting battalion commander during a temporary absence of the major.

second. We lined them up on the road and made a close inspection of equipment.

It was surprising even in a well-equipped company how many little things were lacking here and there—now that the actual test had come. I stripped one or two men in the other platoons of their ammunition in order to supply missing clips where they were necessary, picked out the best automatic rifles and extra magazines; changed a few rifles which were rather suspect, and made one or two shifts in the personnel. In ten minutes the chosen platoon was ready. Then we told the men what was before them.

Instantly the lads of the other platoons crowded around and for a minute or two there was a great handshaking, exchange of keepsakes and little notes —"Mail that to Bess, will you, Jim, and write them home. . . ." There was a spirit and enthusiasm, and yet a realization and lack of sentimentality about it that was fine to see. The men hardly seemed to realize that it was "good-bye" until they were swung into column and actually began to march. Then there was a storm of handshakes and farewells and cheers as they swung up the road to join the platoon from "A" company which had already gone on ahead. Over a third of them never came back. That was one thing you learned at the front; to be glad to see people when you met them, just in case . . .

A few minutes later, after the excitement cooled

down, the main column got under way, and in about an hour we reached our new billet, Le Petit Villiers.

"B" company was lucky at this little town, since we had billets with lots of straw and a barn or so. I found a real house with a fine room for an office, and had the cooker just in front in a cow's "bedroom," that cow having gone the way of all flesh some time previously, to judge by the evidence. We buried her, while the cooks prepared a big meal, with fish for the officers, obtained by throwing a hand grenade in the creek near by—a trick we learned from the French soldiers detailed with us. Then we set up the cots and the company field desk in a room of the old farmhouse which had a pretty view across an orchard, the red roofs of the village peeping over the trees just beyond.

Here the men played baseball at leisure times, and in a field near by one of the companies pitched pup tents, as there were not enough billets to go around. Battalion headquarters took up their office just across the hall, where we could hear their typewriters clicking all day, for even at this time there was a good deal of "paper-work" going on.

Our stay of about a week in this town was a godsend, as during the captain's absence I got the company thoroughly reorganized. Handling 250 men is no joke. I put my "headquarters platoon" in fine shape—mechanics, runners, cooks, and clerks, and appointed some more good non-commissioned officers, of whom there cannot be too many. It seems impossible that Pennsylvania politics could reach to France, even in a guard regiment, but they did. In the old days, a lot of the men had been appointed non-commissioned officers to salve up the folks at home in the fourth ward, or for some such reason, and it was necessary to change this now. I tried to get the right man in the right place.

Very soon the new order of things began to tell.

When a runner left company headquarters for any platoon, things started to happen right way. This was very necessary. We would often get an order to move, and turn out in the middle of the night, carts

harnessed and all loaded, only to have the order countermanded after standing around in the chill of the night for an hour. Sometimes this happened two or three times a night. Few can imagine what this does to the morale of an outfit. Making up packs in pitch darkness, loss of sleep, scrambling and hunting around for things in the dark—as, of course, a light might bring down a bomb, is a real trial. But it finally got to be almost a joke. Soon we could turn out and turn in in no time, and that, I suppose, was what they wanted.

Regimental headquarters at this billet was at an old "farm-château." This was the last place the band played. I went over to see the colonel. He and the adjutant had a room with some of those gigantic beds with funereal urns carved at the top. The big court was full of cows, sheep, chickens, and soldiers, with messengers going and coming. The large headquarters company camped just outside. Officers were shaving under the trees; the cookers were in full blast. Above all other sounds was the incessant noise of wagons, trucks, side cars, and artillery going and coming from the front along the highway near by, one of the great French national routes.

At night the noise of wheels was the most characteristic sound of war-time France. It sounded like a river in flood, washing and rolling its stones over the jagged boulders of its bed. At dawn all this ceased. The wagons were backed into the nearest *bois,* covered with branches and leaves, and the horses tied to trees. All the men disappeared; that is, the French did. The "Yanks" went wandering around like a plumbers' picnic until they had enough men killed off to "get wise." Our military police, the "M.P.'s," directed traffic.

Petit Villiers was a scattered hamlet, two or three disconnected little villages or groups of red-roofed houses among fields and orchards, rambling along green lanes that branched off at various angles from the main road. Battalion headquarters, where we had our company kitchen, was an old stone farmhouse situated on a crossroads about the center of the hamlet. It was here that I slept and had the company office with the field desk. The platoons were billeted on straw in various barns and empty sheds. One platoon was down at the extreme end of the village in a hay-filled barn. But its lieutenant had a real bed, a deep feather bed, in an old peasant's house with spiral stone stairs and heavy black oak rafters. Madame was still living there, dressed in her white cap and *sabots*. She would, if encouraged, bring a little hot water with which to shave. The few chickens about were guarded most jealously, and eggs—an egg was a prize, indeed!

Our men were most forbearing in these billets; very little was ever taken. They seemed to realize that a small flock of chickens, or the scanty milk of an old cow, was perhaps all that a mother and her little family had. With one or two exceptions, in the billets that I saw, the men shared their rations with the French, and every mess line dwindled down at the last to the little tots in wooden shoes. Many a French boy will remember to his dying day the white bread, the sweet American coffee, and the good-natured "Yanks," for in nearly all the villages where we stopped the men were fast friends with the inhabitants, and all the way from Calais until the evacuated zone began, the mail followed us up from the sweethearts along the route behind.

All these little villages were carefully loopholed for machine gun fire. At Petit Villiers, I remember, I took some of the sergeants around to give them a talk on street and village fighting of which so much was going on at the time. At every house on a cross street or lane-end, or from sheds and barns that looked out over the fields, there was a carefully constructed loophole for a machine gun nest, and in some places a concrete and stone covering like a little vault to make it safe from shell fire. Several of the men found a lot of *Chauchat* ammunition hidden in the straw of one of the billets. We thought we had a treasure trove, but it all proved to be defective. Some of the French had probably hidden it to get rid of it on their way to the front. Armies had passed through here.

There was a good deal of air activity also. Balloons and planes were generally visible along the Marne to the eastward. At morning and evening the bombing squadrons went over, going and coming from a raid, flying very high, and filling the air with a pulsing hum of motors. The anti-air barrage at the front was frequent, and occasionally there was a chase and machine gun firing, after an enemy plane.

For the most part, though, everything lay very quiet. The fields dreamed in bright sunshine and summer peace, the men bathed along the cold streams, or drilled in the fields, and only the traffic and uniforms told of war. Each battalion was kept to its own area here by the military police, so the company clerk was worried to death by requests for passes to the Y.M.C.A. canteen, only about a half mile away, but just outside our bounds.

It was here that the two platoons that had gone to the front came back to us. From time to time we had heard rumors about them. The night before their return, a number of their wounded, some in very bad shape, had passed through the regimental hospital on their way to the rear. At last the main body arrived in trucks, about five o'clock one afternoon, just in time for supper formation at which they got a tremendous ovation. About 30 returned to our company out of the 58 who had left. Some 12 of these absentees were known to be wounded; the rest were missing or dead.

These picked platoons had an extraordinary experience, having volunteered to aid the French in an attack on the Germans at Hill 204 near Château-Thierry. Here they met machine guns, hand-to-hand fighting, and several hours of a German barrage. After the battle, the French general at that point of the line took them to his headquarters, complimented them personally, gave them a long-remembered meal, and recommended them all for the *croix de guerre,* which the whole platoon received later on. Lieutenant Shenkel had shot a big, burly German officer, used his own head like a veteran, and was simply idolized by his men. They followed him around like a lot of sheep.

At supper that night the enthusiasm and excitement were at fever heat. Men came from other companies and stood around in tense little circles to hear the wonderful stories "the veterans" had to tell, wonderful but true, and the voices did not die away in the billets till very late.

From this gallant exploit came a spirit that helped us through trials to come. Yet many of those who returned were worn out and unstrung for the strain to come later on. Attrition had already begun its work. There was no one who did not notice how small the second platoon looked.

I was particularly impressed that night by Lieutenant Shenkel. A man who comes out of battle does not get over it for a long time afterward. I went with him that night to his billet, "the billet of the feather bed." While he turned in, I heard the story of the attack on Hill 204. It was a story of agony and pain, of death in the furnace. . . . A wonderful tale, told simply, yet a story of mad adventure. Shenkel was still alive by a series of miracles. His face was flushed, and his eyes wide and brilliant with excitement. He was a different man. Something had come to him which had not yet come to us. It was the trial of battle. No one who passes through that is ever quite the same again.

Toward the Flame

At Petit Villiers drills went on every day while
we lay there. We had a big field and woods in which
to move about and carry out various attack and defense problems. Captain Thorn, who was waiting
to hear from delayed special orders of some weeks
before, laid out several problems. He had one of the
aptest tactical minds I ever ran across, which was
more to the point just then than faultless habits. It
was whispered about that there were several in the
battalion who rather feared his estimate of their own
ability. He was several months waiting for the return of his papers, and at Petit Villiers lived up a
winding staircase in a stone room with a groined ceiling, broken-down furniture, and a candle in a bottle.
I used to sit with him evenings over a little something to eat and drink, when he was really brilliant
at times. His talk flashed around to all points of

the compass,
lighted w i t h
sudden gleams
of humor and
touches of in-
sight, and the
t r u t h that
men tell under
adversity as at
no other time.
Beneath was
a French fam-

ily living in cabinet beds around a kitchen; an elderly woman in granny cap, with heavy seams on each side of her nose, two children, one of the loveliest little girls I have ever seen—like a March rosebud— and her little brother, who used to play house with her in an overturned barrel. Their mother was a soldier's good-looking wife. How they watched the tide of refugees, asking them eager questions as to the news! A slight swaying back and forth of the lines meant life or death then to many a village.

One day a party of officers from the regiment climbed into one of our ration wagons and drove forward ten or twelve kilometers to reconnoiter a new position. It was along the Paris Aqueduct below Château-Thierry, about three miles from the German lines. The nearest town was Nogent-l'Artaud-sur-Marne. We jogged along the good road and stopped where it crossed the aqueduct to go down into the valley, where there was a charming water mill and two men reaping. Just on the other side of the stream lay a dead horse killed by a shell—very evident. Horses lie with their legs in the air, the stiff muscles looking as if they were carved out of wood. The curves of their bodies all grow peculiarly wooden and formal in their rigidity.

We went up on the hill. A party of Italian soldiers was working with the French engineers, getting wood for revetting, fascines, etc., and over on the other side of the hill we could hear an occasional shell whistle and fall with a smash, for the Germans were attempting to shell the working parties along the aqueduct.

I went down to the rear of the mountain with some of the others to see if we could get rations in from that direction. There we found a little village or farm group by a stream where the houses were full of French soldiers eating beans. A sergeant gave me the information I wanted about the roads. I went back and we reconnoitered "the mountain," a curious place.

In peace times there had been a big sand quarry here. A small, narrow-gauge tram track ran all over the hillside, with the rusty cars and engines standing about like a deserted picnic park in the winter. There were several good buildings on the hill, one full of beds which was chosen for battalion headquarters, and one at the very crest which was full of a litter of tools and various cast-off junk. A track ran past it along a green, grass-grown road to a long shed around a curve. I chose this for company headquarters—the fireplace was appealing.

From the aqueduct one could look for miles up and down the Marne. We met General Weigel there and our colonel, and watched Hill 204 vomiting streams of shells at our batteries cleverly placed on the opposite hills. One of the guns was under a big tree on the flats where the Marne made a sharp bend. You could see the nose of it sticking out through the branches, and catch the flash. Every once in a while a great geyser of earth shot up in the air from one of our shells. We were looking at the German lines.

Château-Thierry, a beautiful, white city, lay at the foot of a hill a few miles away, and other towns up and down the river valley. Not a soul could be seen, no wagons on the roads, the railroads only a rusty red line, the towns mere shells. The river flowed down through the hills past the little patches of crops and crimson poppies, white roads and green woods. It was like an inland landscape, a mosaic of grain and garden patches; the church spires like toy towers, and a strange silence over all except for the distant grumble of guns. Every one had fled. It was only the ghost of a world that we were looking at. The Marne twisted through it for miles, and there was always the brilliant sunshine over it—the white French sunshine that seemed almost wrong.

Along the river I found a lot of new trenches the French were digging in case the "Boche" got that far. It was these that we were to occupy as a support line. In fact, the whole mountain was to be a strong-point. We laid it out, fields of fire, machine gun support, company sectors and all. Sometimes I feel sorry that the enemy did not try to take it; it was such a little Gibraltar. What surprised us though was the small number of men assigned to defend it.

21

Toward the Flame

The French soldiery left everything they touched
dirty. All the woods were full of little bowers and
rustic seats littered with refuse, cast-off clothes, ammunition cans, excrement, and old rifles. Little
signs tagged various places *"Villa Bon Air," "Château Incroyable,"* etc. The paths were wired with
a hand wire so you could follow them in the dark
—very necessary—and labeled *"Chemin de Ronde,"
"Avenue de l'Etoile,"* and so forth.

Near the road I found a haunted little place, white
pebbles and garden walks with the print of big feet
in the flower beds. At one side was a wrecked dolls'
house and smashed dishes—a whole symbol of what
had overtaken civilization. I looked at the marks of
the big military boots among the crushed flowers.
I hope the owners have come back to take tea.

There were other interesting things about this
place, too. Near a well by a bridge was a cluster of
houses, just on "our side" of Nogent, numerous little
villas with cast-iron gates and gable roofs. One of
them had a court with a rather quaint warehouse on
one side. They had once packed moss there for
Christmas, and dyed it green. There were tons of
it. I do not doubt that we have bought some of it at
home. The business had been a prosperous one, as
the house was full of fine and tasteful things. It had
been looted, of course, and the safe shot full of holes.
Account books, old photographs, clothes, wrecked
chairs, letters, pieces of the splintered building, and

coats with their sleeves out, lay all about the floors and up and down the stairs. A litter of soldiers' cooking added the last fine, little touch.

There were thousands and thousands of houses like that in France. All the quiet, tender privacies of family life turned out naked and shrieking to the gaze of all. I billeted a platoon here where they slept on the green dyed moss, but that was a day or so later.

Just across the bridge was a big farm with one of those enormous barns the French build. They were still getting in the harvest here, and there were some children playing about with gas masks hanging at their sides. It was here too that the wagon waited for us and we went back to Petit Villiers.

On the way down, a boy jumped onto the wagon with us and rode for a while. He was going home from his aunt's farm. In his particular commune of Belleville there had been no school for two years. He could read only what "mamma had taught." The school was full of wounded. A very apt lad growing up ignorant. No wonder war makes people more religious!

The schoolmaster came around and dined with us at Petit Villiers. He was a sad, fat man with his hair parted in the middle, who spoke a little intensely grammatical English. Lunch was served out in the open in front of a French house, on some boards laid over a couple of saw horses. No cheese could be had here. Each billet nearer the front saw some luxury cut off the dwindling list.

That night we left Petit Villiers hours before dawn. The companies lined up in the dim moonlight, with a child crying somewhere away off. There was a devil of a mess at the road forks with an artillery regiment trying to get ahead of us. I think this was the evening of July the Fourth, 1918.

The men said we always moved on a holiday.

CHAPTER II

BEHIND THE FRONT

AFTER leaving Petit Villiers we marched four or five kilometers, got near a large farm that was to have been our next billet, and found that some other organization had arrived there ahead of us. It was a mistake on their part as they had been assigned to another place, but that was cold comfort to us. The whole battalion turned around like a snake, marched back a little, and finally lay down right along the road in a ditch and slept. Nick, my good Italian striker, filled our portion of the gutter with grass and hay, and we huddled up in it to keep warm.

It is on such nights as this that one really sees the stars. To lie and look up at them is to become more sane. Somehow they always filled me with confidence. Perhaps that is why generals took to wearing them.

Next morning we got up from the roadside, rather stiff, and moved over to two big farms, during which time it rained violently. "A" company went into one large barn, and "B" company into another, with some crowding, and a remonstrance on the part of the owner who was an old Alsatian and spoke German. For that reason he got hustled for a while, until I stopped it and explained the matter to the men.

A French farm in the country north of Paris is simply an immense building around a court. It is at once a dwelling, barn, lofts, stables, etc., with a manure heap of vast and nauseating proportions in the center. We got the boys out of the streaming rain, took away the ladders from the lofts, to keep them from wandering, and started the cooker. Lieutenant Shenkel and I found a dark little room next to another hole in the wall where an immense sow lived. She stuck her nose through to be fed, petted, or teased. When the sun came out, the manure heap smoked intolerably; my nails were so full of dirt as to be a source of pain; the fires went out—and mess was delayed.

A little later I went across to "A" company to see Captain Williams. I was standing by "his" barn,

26

when General King's car came around the corner, plumped down an absentee that the general had picked up, and disgorged the general himself very "wrathy." "Send for Captain Williams at once— why did he let his men wander all over France like that?" etc., etc. The wrath of God also fell on me, as a man passed just then with a Red Cross sweater worn on the outside of his shirt. The general, however, was really reasonable enough and must have appreciated the kind of night we had been through. It was necessary to have some one to keep the lid on. I saluted and discreetly vanished.

By this time the mud was eighteen feet deep—at least. I floundered home to my bedroom next to the sow's and found that I was invited to lunch by the farmer's wife, in the coziest little beechwood room all glistening with copper kettles and pewter. We had fried eggs and cheese, salad, and a bottle of some fiery, liquor, offered with much pride. I sent out to our mess sergeant and got some coffee and white bread for my hosts. Fraternity reigned. The children and flies were in a dead heat for the molasses when they brought us an order to move.

A big pile of clothes had just been brought in a few minutes before. I had sent back our carts to get them at Petit Villiers. These clothes began to be a joke or a *hoodoo*. Every time they appeared, we immediately moved before they could be issued. The men fell in after a wild scramble for "size 6" or

a "32-27." Some were especially loath to leave, as
they really needed a change, so the first sergeant had
to resort to a little persuasion. In his own language
he "had to rap a few birds." Then order came at
last. We sloshed down the muddy road with our
boots sucking. I could see them creasing white
trousers at West Point!

There was a long march that day, passing over a
causeway that ran for miles over a shallow lake. At
one place, where we stopped, a peasant and his little
boy were fishing for frogs, with hooks and a red flan-
nel bait. The shadows of the willows lay very clear
on the ponds, and music from the band of one of the
other regiments came across the water. You could
hear the trumpets and drums.

At last we got out of this swamp country and
camped in a sort of open grove. The colonel called
the officers around him and read the congratulations
of the French general and the orders from the division about our two platoons. There were fires going
here, and singing, as we were far enough away to do
that. Next day we marched again toward the hill
we had reconnoitered some time before, and camped
in a wood about two miles behind it.

We lay there for a week, long enough to get the
woods into living shape. The men pitched pup tents,
and I had a bower made for me. Nick had learned
to make baskets in Italy and he wove me a wonderful
little house. I paid the company off here under the

trees, a tremendous job—all in French money with change very scarce. Crap games immediately started. There was no place to spend money except an occasional Y.M.C.A. canteen. When these came around, chocolate, cigarettes, little pasteboard boxes of jam, matches and various other Christian luxuries appeared, nor must I forget to mention the little packages of cakes so much desired. It was like being a child again.

One day the colonel drove up to our entrance to the woods, called for Shenkel, and told him to get his stuff together right away as he was to be sent home to train troops, and promoted captain. He was a little bit dazed by good fortune, but he packed his stuff, and the men got in line to say good-bye. In the green light under the trees they filed by, shaking hands and not saying very much.

Shenkel was a terrible loss to the company, our only other lieutenant was off on detached service with the Ninth Infantry at this time, which left me the only officer with the company. The captain was still commanding the battalion. Living as close to them as I had to do in the woods, the men nearly nagged me to death. Robin Hood must have had his nerves shattered by forest intimacies.

A few nights later we moved to our assigned position on the hill. The men were placed on duty where they could turn out to man the trenches and strongpoints quickly. I got my little house at the top of the hill cleaned out and a fire started in the fireplace, with blankets over the windows. The cooker was hidden under an old shed with a cast iron roof. Most of the men were housed and the rest camped in the woods. Battalion headquarters had the big stone house and was quite comfortable. Shells fell here at night, but in well-defined localities, and a gas bombardment came over regularly every morning about three o'clock. We got some old brass shells and mounted them for alarms. This was really a joke, as there was never enough gas to amount to anything. Alarms were frequent, nevertheless, as the men were nervous and overtrained in "gas."

"Fritz" was gunning steadily for the bridge at Nogent. Every three minutes a shell whistled down the valley. It often fell within a few feet of the bridge or in the town, yet it never quite hit the target.

The nerve strain began here, though. We had all kinds of alarms and stand-to's, as at that time the Germans were expected to start a new drive, and we were to be in position if it came. We raced up and down the hill at all hours of the day and night. "The situation has changed" became a joke, but for the most part things were quiet in the daytime.

I used to slip down and see the platoon that was housed in the moss factory. The men had the place halfway clean as the major general had lately visited us, and they could be found sleeping or sitting along the wall cleaning their rifles. There would be groups scattered about at one kind of gambling game or another. Some were reading, some cooking small potatoes they had dug themselves, mixed with a few beans, some shaving and washing, while others wrote home. The guard reliefs kept passing in and out, and a lot of good-natured banter and tales of "things I used to do at home" passed around. Lines of packs stood against the walls made up ready to move, the "U.S." staring from the flaps.

I went over into Nogent, about a mile away, one day, with Paul, one of the French soldiers attached to our company—eighteen of them were assigned to the battalion. I made friends with them and got them all attached to "B" company for rations.* They

* This permitted "B" company to draw eighteen additional rations.

31

helped a lot, giving me sound advice and helping the cooks. Their sergeant major was a fine fellow, proud as a turkey cock, and justly so. He knew what all the "Boche" flares meant, and so really saved me one night from walking over into "Fritz's" front yard.

So Paul and I went into Nogent.

The place had been shelled and deserted. I am not going to describe it, as all these shelled towns were more or less the same. Each, however, had its own phase of tragedy. One touch here I remember: In a bedroom, as we went in, a huge cat rose on the lace-covered bed, arching her back, bottle-tailed; on the floor were two small high-heeled shoes. Nogent was not in such bad shape, just shot up generally. A school had been hit horribly.*

We went up to what had been the restaurant at the station and crawled in the back way. The shutters were closed, and about twenty-five French soldiers were sitting around drinking. Some one had brought in the big, wax, funeral candles from the undertaker's opposite, and there was an unexpected yellow illumination as one entered the room. Paul explained my extreme affection for the French and hinted at the possibility of my supplying some white bread. Madame, a rather fat but still handsome woman, in a coarse way, came forward followed by a French sergeant who was evidently living on and with her. There was much talk, handshaking and

* See the author's poem, *The Blindman.*

smiles, a few toasts and Madame's story over a bottle of wine.

She is the last woman in the place. Trade is gone and tomorrow she leaves. Her husband and two sons are dead—army, of course—there is nothing to live for. This is the second time in four years that the town has been wrecked.

French soldiers knocked and stamped in and out. There was a parley at the door each time, as if we were in a lodge, on account of the M.P.'s being near by. I told her of the American Red Cross where refugees could get help, while she gave me some eggs, cheese, two bottles of excellent wine, and a huge fish, killed by the Germans shelling the river, still fresh. The shells bursting in the Marne brought everything up for a long way. There was a great furor at the officers' mess when I got back to camp, and admonitions about not wandering off—over the fish and wine. The major returned from school here and took charge, but what was much more important to me, I got a real hot bath.

There was an old iron bathtub under a sand shed. I got Nick to heat some water by building a fire under the tub, and after it cooled off considerably, I had a "terribly" hot bath, coming out like new into the cold night after a brisk rub, then clean clothes. The old ones I buried.

We got an order to move that night, which was later countermanded after we had lain about under arms in the rain. Messing around, I found a cross over a mock grave with "4th Infantry" carved on it, so I knew my friend Francis Hogan, who was in that regiment, was not very far off.

We moved at noon—very hot—and marched across fields by an ancient signal tower left over from Napoleon's time, when news was semaphored across France. At last we hit the paved road and passed through a little town where the two colonels and the general of our brigade saw us go by. A lot of weary men, too tired to answer the usual, "What outfit, boys?" soon passed us going towards the rear. The platoons looked small. They had been at the front. We could hear artillery constantly, and in the full heat of the afternoon passed through a badly shelled town. One stream of troops was going one way, and one another. A big relief was in progress. The dust simply smoked, and we got almost too tired to get out of the way of trucks. We arrived in the town and halted while some French soldiers brought us water from the wells. They would not let our own men leave ranks in the village. The road was lined with artillery farther on, 75's firing now and then. We would get the flash, the blast of air, and the blow of sound every minute or so.

About five o'clock we moved into a wood. The men lay right down where they were, some stripped, and all slept. I went back to locate our cooker and waited for it to turn up among the rest of the traffic at the crossroads. I fell to talking with the M.P. there, a big, competent fellow who handled the traffic professionally. While we were talking, there came a droning sound. Some instinct moved us off the road down behind a field dyke. There was a crash like the world's end; dirt and stones like a landslide. Everybody falls prone at a time like that. Then we got up and looked. Just where we had been talking was a pit about four feet deep still smoking. The French came along and put a cartload of stone in it right away, and the ambulances that had been held up began streaming past immediately. Our own cooker came up at last and we had supper quickly— the last cooked meal we got for a long time. As it was, we scarcely got that.

The major hustled us off in column of file about twilight. We marched and turned and twisted, scouts being at the corners for part of the way. The captain had gone ahead with some of the other officers to locate our position. All that I knew was that we were to relieve the 30th U. S. Infantry.

The earth and air trembled with artillery. We did not know it, but one of the greatest barrages that had ever been thrown, up to that time, was being put over by the Germans. Planes were fighting overhead, their machine guns flashing like fireflies. I remember passing a shelled farm where our boys were drawing water and smoking. Lots of trucks passed us, but pretty soon we wound out onto a moonlit

35

tableland, over the edge of which we could see the great red and white German flares going up together with all kinds of rockets.

A right-angle turn brought us to a sepulchral village, where there were a few gleams of light from a ration dump.

Some one gave a false gas alarm here. The men put on their masks needlessly, and the two rear platoons got confused and went up the wrong road. Men kept yelling, "Gas! gas!" I found myself with only two platoons, out on an earthen causeway, headed toward an unknown woods across gas-smelling fields, with shells falling ahead. I got the sergeants to go down the line to stop the men calling "gas!" and got the masks off. I ran back myself and got the last two platoons back in line, holding up the company to do it. In ten minutes we were an army again; for a while confusion had made us a mob. Several men dropped out, done out or frightened. I made the rest close up to keep *liaison*.

We moved on about a mile when I got news from the front of the line, after a long halt, that "A" company had lost its front platoon and had no officers. This meant that the leading platoon of the column had marched on with the guide and left us. The chain was broken at the first link. I was the only officer with "B," and it was a long way rearward to "C" company. I sent a runner back to Captain Haller to tell him that I had gone ahead, and took a hard-

headed Forest County lad along with me to find out
the lay of the land. We searched a most desolate
stretch of country for an hour, but could find nothing—only woods ahead. Finally I walked a long
distance and came across a main road lined with
poplars.

Bullets were droning through the trees now and
then and the road was full of cut limbs and branches.
I was very much frightened by this time and did not
even know where the enemy lay, except generally.
Finally I found a telephone station at a crossroads,
and two men. They were sleeping, and one was a
useless Italian. I threw some water over the opera-
tor from a bucket that was standing there, and
rustled him around generally till he got thoroughly
awake and could react consciously. He took me
down the road about five hundred yards to a place
called Fossoy, where there was a regimental headquarters, a famous old regular outfit, the Seventh
U. S. Infantry.

The officer on duty was just coming from the
latrine and desired to be sociable. He asked me
where the regiment came from and wanted to know
if I knew somebody in Pittsburgh. In the meantime, the whole battalion was lying out in shell fire
while this went on. It seemed impossible to get any
definite information. This is just the way things
happen. Men cannot realize the true situation, especially at night or after great fatigue, and some never

at all. Finally I made out that I had gone too far, a whole regiment to the left, the regiment we were to relieve was along the Paris road "somewhere," and that was all they knew. I blessed them and departed.

It was very dark now; the moon had set. I got back to the battalion, all lying down sleeping, and then went along the Paris road down into a woods where the trees were all cut off by artillery fire about eight feet up. The white flares that went up from the enemy lines showed me that it was full of dead men in all conceivable contortions. Some had been blown to pieces two or three times; others lay as if asleep; some were just torsos. There was a head with glasses still on. The gas masks added the last

devilish effect. Up the road a little I stumbled over a dead mule and caught myself on its stiff leg. Here I was ghastly sick of heart and body for a while. But I managed to get on and at last came to a battalion headquarters sign at a little crossroads, where there were a lot of horses lying dead and already badly swollen. In the ground, a few yards away, I saw a very faint gleam of light. I walked over toward it, and found that it came from a dugout, which I entered and tramped on a knot of sleeping men. The place was full of gas, and those in it dead from sleep.

I learned that battalion headquarters was in another dugout next door, so I went up and then down another stairs, and finally into a lantern-lit cave full of vile air and packed with men. It was a hole in the earth banked and covered by logs, with a steep pitching stairway of mud. The major's eyes looked like a pink rabbit's from lack of sleep, and he talked thick and low. That our battalion was lost could mean nothing to him. He gave me a guide, who, after being awakened with the greatest of difficulty, took me out and lost me. I got back in half an hour and found our battalion scout officer. We went up and found our own battalion. It had moved forward some and the head of it was in the woods. We had an officer from the 30th U. S. Infantry for a guide by this time and got our whole outfit into the woods, waking the men with great difficulty. In a few minutes there was daylight and we would have been in full view of the German batteries and machine guns. We were on one side of the valley and the "Boche" on the other. Fighting was going on in the towns that lay between. It sounded like riveting in a boiler.

The Germans had planned a great drive up this

valley from Château-Thierry and had laid down suddenly the greatest barrage in history up to that time —greater than any at Verdun.* For many square miles there was a shell-hole everywhere, every few feet. It was this frightful fire that had caught whole regiments of our men living in bowers in the woods. They were swept out, one regiment particularly, that which we were relieving. Theirs were the dead men that I had seen, and had we come an hour or so earlier, we should have been caught, too.

The litter through those woods was unimaginable to any one who never saw its like. There was one cheerful thing about it, though. One hour before the Germans started their great drive for Paris, Marshal Foch started his for Berlin. Our artillery and machine guns caught the Germans in column of squads on pontoons on the Marne. Hundreds were killed, and in the valley near Château-Thierry, where lie the little towns of Crézancy and Connigis, a Yankee regiment, the 39th Infantry Regulars, stopped the Boche.

The French left their guns, by order, and our boys got in the harness and hauled the 75's forward to point-blank range and fired them like machine guns, loading on the recoil. It was there that the last German drive for Paris was stopped, the high water mark of the 1918 Teuton flood.

After that the tide was on the ebb.

* This was what we were told and believed at the time.

CHAPTER III

IN THE VALLEY OF THE SHADOW

INTO the valley, a few hours after the worst was over, we came, filing down the mountainside in single file, the whole battalion stretched out for a mile or two. Because no one would have expected us to do such a thing, we got in. I looked back at several places and saw the snake-like line filing down and down in the dusk of the morning.

Near the bottom of a hill we found some of the 30th Infantry lying in a sunken road along the Paris Aqueduct, our old friend bobbing up again. Captain Law had met us by this time, and we sheltered the men as best we could. The place was rotten with vomiting gas. It is easy to imagine what took place. There was some tear gas, too. Some of the men we put in an old trench the engineers had dug, others in the sunken road, and still others in defilade space * as near as I could find it. The rest of the battalion was strung out along the aqueduct in little valleys where some started to dig in.

I tried to use all the brains I had in getting shelter, and found a little arroyo about four or five feet deep without a single shell mark. It seemed to be out of the line of fire. I got Nick to pitch my tent in this, and the "top sergeant" crawled in with me. The headquarters platoon camped near by. You must imagine a lot of holes in the earth down a water course, with canvas over them, covered by leaves.

The captain went back to the major's dugout about a quarter of a mile up the hill. Some of the boys dug in deep. Next morning I went down to the aqueduct and broke into a man-hole with some of the men, washed, shaved, and got the mustard gas off me. The whole side of the hill was alive with soldiers. The place looked like an ant heap. Men were coming along the aqueduct with clinking canteens strung on poles and waiting in line at the man-holes to fill them. None of us knew exactly where we were or what to expect. Several airplanes flew over us,

* Protected position out of line of fire.

among them some enemy planes. The enemy had the mastery of the air at this point; only a few of our planes ever came near us.

It was a fine warm morning, and I went back and crawled under my tent to sleep for the first time in two days, first starting a detail up the hill for rations. About five o'clock our batteries woke me up. I found our hill was surrounded by batteries hidden on the crest, mostly 75's. Each one had a sound of its own; one seemed to ring like a bell, and a nearer one shook us with its explosion, while still another seemed to bark. They were fighting batteries across the Marne about eight or ten miles away.

Pretty soon German shells began to come back, falling in line, but short. The worst thing was that every shell fell in the woods where our men were. We had a number wounded before dark. About dusk we began to get three or four shells every minute or so. The men left the areas where they fell, and we turned in. It was pitch dark. The first sergeant and I lay together in our little dugout in the watercourse. We were safe from everything but a direct hit. To be shelled is the worst thing in the world. It is impossible to imagine it adequately. In absolute darkness we simply lay and trembled from sheer nerve tension.

There is a faraway moan that grows to a scream, then a roar like a train, followed by a ground-shaking smash and a diabolical red light. In the valley the echoes were tremendous. About eleven o'clock the range shifted and shell after shell fell directly among the men—the most awful screams and moans —cries for stretchers from "C" company. We couldn't find where they were in the dark.

Let me remark that if you are one of those who think everybody is brave under shell fire like that, you are wrong. "Everybody" simply shakes and crawls. Of course, you go out and do what you can. All this was simply a fight between the batteries: "Yesterday all was quiet along the front except for intermittent artillery duels," says the *communiqué*.

In the Valley of the Shadow

Thank God! few can know what that really means.

Our batteries were throwing over ten to one. There would be a half hour of quiet; then whistle—smash—another shell from "Jerry"; then our batteries barking like a lot of savage dogs, with the howls of our own shells; rockets, falling trees, screams, the flop-flop of gas shells; white-faced men digging like mad or standing up under it according to their temperament—some cool, some shaking, some weeping; a few grim jokes, but mostly just dull endurance; a hunching of the shoulders when another comes, and the thought—"How long, how long?" There is nothing to do. Whether you get through or not is just sheer chance and nothing more. You may and you may not. *C'est la guerre.*

We stayed in that place—the men called it Death Valley—for five days. I will not give a diary of it, only one or two things.

In the morning we went around collecting the dead. It was necessary to collect individuals blown to pieces as well as whole men. The last two days some of the men dug for me and the first sergeant a hole between two layers of stone that went directly into the sheer face of a hill about 500 feet high. There was sand between the two layers about four feet apart. The last two nights I slept, secure myself, with some of the men who were not able to stand it out in the open any longer. By that time everybody had dug in pretty well.

Toward the Flame

One morning a French major with an American captain came down the hill, asking for various items of information. He had all necessary credentials and had passed through battalion headquarters. He got sketches of our positions. About an hour later a lieutenant came down from regimental headquarters with orders to arrest him. He was a German spy. Both of them were, I feel sure, although the "American captain" must have lived a long time in the United States as his accent was quite natural and he was familiar with the streets in my home town.

Owing to this visit, the bombardment that night was deadly and accurate. I tried to get Captain Law to shift the men out of a trench the fourth platoon occupied, but he could not see the advantage of leaving cover to move forward into the open. About two o'clock a poor "kid" came to my dugout, evidently with something to say, but he couldn't say it. He led me over to the fourth platoon trench. We hit the ground about every thirty seconds. They had the trench "cold"; the place was full of dead and wounded. Three direct hits had accounted for fifteen.*

I was so frightened myself, I could scarcely get the men together. One sergeant, cool as a cucumber, came up and gave me an immense sense of help. There were three or four maniacs from shell shock whom we had to overpower. We dug some of the

---

* These men were not all killed.

46

poor devils out and started them up the hill. The faint sounds and stirrings in the caved-in banks were terrible. Some we could not reach in time, and one of these was smothered. We had one party of wounded all together and started up the hill once, when a big shell fell right in their midst. I saw men blown into the air. Awful confusion again. . . . The state of a wounded man, wounded again, and still under fire, is beyond description.

Two more shells hit the trench, and I sent the men forward two or three hundred yards. They were in perfect safety there, all shells sailing over them.

We got what wounded we could and dragged them up to battalion headquarters. There were no stretch-ers there, and I  could not get any one to come out of the dugouts. I shouted at them, but heard only muffled voices in reply. The darkness was inky. One of the men was hit again.

That was the first time in my life that I ever knew what it was to be angry. If certain of the men in the dugouts had come out then I believe I could have shot at them. Lieutenant Sharpe, the scout officer, who was the only one there who tried to do anything for us, finally got a runner to send up to the dressing station and ask for stretchers.

Sharpe and I in the meantime tried to bandage some of the poor devils. The feel of warm human bodies and blood, the quiet patience and confidence of the men, brought a realization of life to me in that hour that I shall never forget. "This is my body which is given for you." What that really meant, now I knew.

After half an hour the stretcher bearers came and the men were taken up and borne away.

Going down the hill again, I got the nearest call; a "big boy" came over and exploded in a drain beside the road. I had thrown myself down, of course, but I got tossed and wafted some feet in sliding débris. Nothing hit me. I went back to Sergeant Davidson in the dugout after a while with a numb feeling in my side, pretty well unnerved and shaken up. Nick made me some hot coffee over an alcohol lamp. I slept after a while, and next day came to, rather than woke up, about eleven o'clock—beautiful sunshine—it hardly seemed possible in those woods.

Lieutenant Glendenning and I took some men and went back to the fourth platoon trench. We took shelter halves and blankets and went through the ditch and picked up arms and hands and everything else. Some things we just turned under, and the most we buried in a great shell-hole. Then we pulled out the men that were smothered in the dirt; some were cut in pieces by the shell fragments and came apart when we pulled them out of the bank. Lieutenant Quinn, a Pittsburgh boy, who had just got his commission a week before,* was so mixed with the two men who had lain nearest to him that I do not know yet whether we got things just right. But we made three graves, and buried them in a very well-marked position, one man on each side of the lieutenant, just as they had died, between stones 132 and 133 on the Paris Aqueduct, looking toward, and opposite the town of Connigis across the valley. A Catholic priest, one of our chaplains, came and said a few words, some of the boys knelt and it was all over. I got Quinn's watch, which was *still going,* and gave it to his brother a few weeks later on.

We did not feel this so much at the time. Trying to get the identification tags is the worst, but you get numbed after a while.

I took the priest up to my dugout. We had lunch, hot, and he gave me some cigarettes and tobacco. He was a human being. We talked for a long while about Rome, which he knew well. That was a great rest. Nick came in beaming to hear talk of his be-

---

* Quinn's promotion was a fatal one. A shell exploded exactly opposite the platoon commander's dugout.

49

loved Italy; told us about the chestnuts roasting in the ashes, and the girls' cheeks growing red in wintertime at home. About five o'clock they started to shell again.

One night I went out on the side of the hill to establish an observation post where there was a sweeping view up and down the valley. That was the first place where I really got an idea what a big quarrel the war was. For miles and miles the crests that extended back and back were lined with cannon, all flashing and rumbling, too far away to hear except like a far-off storm. Clear over the horizon the glare showed like a steel converter, but shaking and licking halfway across the sky. The valley which was otherwise quiet and lovely, with white villages and roads, had a sound in it like a great electric fan pulsing and pulsing, and there were little lights flashing and winking as if an invisible traffic were passing. These were the shells with tracers, sailing down to Château-Thierry and the heights beyond, where there was an eternal red winking as they burst, too far off to sound. Foch was blasting the enemy loose.

There was no answer coming back.

Along the aqueduct, a little to the west of our position, one of our aviators had been shot down. He had evidently been trying to make a get-away and had lost control and swooped down among the trees. The plane lay with its tail caught in the branches, hung up like a gigantic mottled squid. The front was all smashed, but the aviator was sitting in his chair burned to death. There was nothing left of him but a blackened, egg-shaped mass, his arms and legs having been burned away. The buttons, the hobnails of his shoes, and a few other unburnable things were scattered about the wreck of his machine, and there was a throat-tightening stench of seared flesh. We tried to get his tag but could not find it.

One of the captains of the 30th knew that Lieutenant Roosevelt had been shot down near by so we did our best to identify this man, but without result. That he was an American, we knew by his buttons. He had evidently been on a bombing expedition, for there was a whole drift of bombs lying together on the bank in front of the plane. We steered very clear of them. A party from the 30th Infantry buried him, I heard later on.

One afternoon I got orders to lead a combat patrol to a town called Crézancy about three miles down the valley nearer the Marne. We were to occupy it that night with two platoons. I left with about twelve men and carried a rifle myself. We went down a sunken road and out of the rotten, gassed woods into the blessed sunshine. The Germans were supposed to be just across the valley, about a mile away, so we went single file, keeping a good background of field for long enough to be sure we were not under observation. Then we took the road under the poplar trees and moved fast.

Toward the Flame

It was the big, straight highroad down the valley, macadamized, and covered with a litter of branches from shell-struck trees. Little villages we sneaked upon, but they were empty—simply eggshells of houses shelled to pieces, a few pigeons still about. At one place we passed a wrecked Ford with a man lying in the ditch beside it, without any head. Everybody was in high spirits at getting into the light and air, and I am afraid the headless man was rather humorously dealt with.

We came into the town of Cresanzy by way of a watercourse and an old springhouse, and nearly scared the heart out of one of our own pickets, who was much astonished at our advent. Every move like that convinced me that the thing to do was the unusual. It is always a surprise, and worked on the enemy as well as it did on our own men. In this case "F" and "E" companies of my own regiment, or some of their platoons, were already in the town.

Crézancy is, or was, a good-sized, prosperous and delightful little town. It had been shelled and reoccupied twice by both sides. The streets were full of slate and bricks, fires burning here and there, walls full of holes. The church was ripped open on one side, but not much hurt on the interior, where a great oil painting of the Passion hung. The bell lay on its side in the tower, lolling out its clatter like a dog's tongue. All windows were smashed, furniture and all manner of articles wasted around, and a kind of breathless air of dead expectancy hung over the place. When one moved through the streets there was a little crackle of slate and tinkle of broken glass under the heavy footfalls.

We met a moving picture man here—where we had expected to meet the enemy—war is full of surprises. A lot of our men were living in cellars, scattered about. They took me to what had been a fine club of some kind with big vaults for wine. Here Lieutenant Frank Mehrton, a good friend of mine, had his command post. He and some other officers of the old regiment were eating in the dining room, blankets over the windows and candles aglow.

This was a magnificent room. It boasted a huge chandelier, oak wainscoting, and leather screens, wonderful upholstered chairs, and a silver service which "Fritz" had had to leave in order to get out of the town quickly enough when our troops moved in.

The joke of it was that he had left a great supply of food, too. The club had evidently been a regimental headquarters. We had an excellent meal cooked in a big chafing dish with griffins on it. All kinds of things, tinned but succulent, were plentiful. The wine was a godsend. In the midst of the festivities the alcohol slopped over and started a fire that threatened to envelop the sideboard for a minute or two. Mehrton's platoon had come through an awful baptism also, and we toasted each other, after a manner, on still being alive. He had been at the Langres School of Arms some months before with me.

I turned the men loose for half an hour "to root," gave a rendezvous, and started with my sergeants to lay out our positions for the two platoons that were to come and occupy the town. It took us all of two hours to do that. The place could have been defended wonderfully, as there were trenches and strong-points already built.

I then went over and connected with the 39th U. S. Infantry at a little town called Moulin, on the right of our position. There was a machine gun outfit there, and a company of infantry. Another battalion was nonchalantly stringing through the place in single file, advancing to the attack; you could hear rifle fire about a quarter of a mile way.

At Moulin I met a captain, who told me the usual story about the losses in his outfit, and in those days they were only too true. He showed me the coat of a surgeon who had been sniped that morning. He was standing at the door of his cellar when some German got the telescopic sight on him. He must have laid the cross-wires in the sight over the cross on the doctor's arm. The bullet struck dead in the center of the cross and came out at the doctor's neck. He lived long enough very calmly to transfer some records and dictate a little letter home. I should like to have seen that letter.

In the Valley of the Shadow

The captain made arrangements to exchange runners with me. I showed him my plan of defense, and left just in time to see our men drive the Germans over the edge of the hill near by. It was like an Indian fight, sniping, crawling, rushing, and then suddenly they had them on the run. I heard our machine guns burst out on the other side of the hill; their chattering echoed up and down the valley. *Finis Fritz*. That was his last stand west of the Marne. Just a few snipers that had been left behind.

Part of the garrison at Crézancy was living in the old railroad station with about fifty beds in the cellar. One of the first things that happens in an occupied town is that the men go out and gather in all of the mattresses. Most dugouts that "Fritz" left were well provided. In order to keep from drawing a shelling, the men had not moved anything in the yard. There was a child's bicycle by the station and a little wagon. To have moved these would have shown up in aerial photos and might have brought a bombardment on that part of the town. One learned quite a few wrinkles like that by bitter experience.

I went back through the town, after carefully laying out an old ruined farm on the flank as part of our scheme of defense. There was water there, good shelter, and a fine flanking field of fire, had "Fritz" cared to try to come back again. Uptown there was a whole quartermaster dump abandoned. We stripped and got new clothes from head to foot; the men got new rifles; everything was plentiful. It was like Christmas.

In what had been the big school I found the Red Cross stores: boxes of tobacco, chocolate, paper, typewriters, etc., etc., all half looted. I think the quartermaster, Red Cross, and Y.M.C.A. stores were all mixed and cluttered together here. We took our needs and tried to carry a little extra back for the boys in the woods. Upstairs there were some delightful prints on the walls, old ones. I wanted one, but it would have been folly to have carried it away with no chance to preserve it. One had no compunction about taking things in these towns, as they were doomed. There was a quiet bedroom here with a gentleman's outfit in it; the curtains were blowing in and out at the windows. Some one sat in the chair. The droop of the jaw was not to be mistaken. Half his back was shot away.

In the Valley of the Shadow

In the courtyard there was a ruined brick tower, a litter of all known things, and two gassed horses, their ribs sticking out like death and a white mucus coming out of their blind eyes. They went around nosing for water and bleating in their throats.

Every house in these ruined towns was a story in itself, a tragedy. I shall tell you about some other places later on and leave Crézancy. About six o'clock one of our company buglers found me and told me to rejoin the company, as Crézancy was to be reoccupied by another regiment and ours was on the move. So all our little scouting expedition and plans were in vain, but it had been a nice little adventure.

We got back into the woods just in time to get into a gas bombardment of about ten minutes' duration. Our first platoon got the worst dose and the men suffered intensely as we moved up out of the woods in single file; just as we had moved into them, in fact. One of the greatest trials was having to march gassed men when there was nothing else to be done, although sometimes it was fatal.

We stirred up a lot of mustard gas getting out, and had the usual trouble of alarms and men getting lost when they put their masks on. Brown, one of "B" company's sergeants, who was born on the Brandywine in Pennsylvania and had spent nearly all his life in the country and woods, led us out by a short cut that avoided the shelled areas.

Our scout officer thought we were lost and came

up the line to stop us. He begged us in that intense way that men do who are sure they are right and know that they have no chance of being believed. He was sadly unstrung from the strain, and it took us a few minutes to assure him that we knew what we were doing. Our commanding officers had lost us so often that his scepticism was to be condoned.

After a while we came out onto the plateau above into moonlight and pure air. A new spirit, one of relief and release, seized us; we were free from that death-hole at last! A mile or so took us past an old château with a few gleams of lights about it. There was a ration dump there, regimental headquarters; autos were droning faintly on the road and men moving about freely. Death was not looking over our shoulder any more.

CHAPTER IV

THE MARCH TO CHÂTEAU-THIERRY

THE march that night was a killer. We lay about on the roads for a while letting a lot of machine gun outfits pass us with their little horse carts like Indian sledges made out of poles with the tribal goods piled on them. Everybody was asking everybody else where we were going, and nobody knew.

There was a mist with the queer, frosty effect of the moonlight on it, and through this, along the glimmering roads, the endless train of men and carts passed, dim, muffled figures with the glow of a pipe or cigarette lighting up a face now and then. Sometimes there would be a halt and the impatient stamping and kicking of horses; a low-toned conversation, then the grinding and rutting ahead that told that the move was on again, and the indistinct column would move forward into the wall of mist. It was getting cold.

We moved out over the plateau. Every wood had its battery, and it was here for the first time we ran across our own divisional artillery. In front of every patch of trees was the marker lantern glowing like a wet firefly in the grass. You could hear the snorting, grinding trucks going and coming back and forth making the nightly trips for supply and ammunition. We stood aside on many a muddy stretch to let them thrash by.

The gassed men gave us great trouble, especially when it came on to rain. We moved on, crept, dragging the gasping gas cases along with us, carrying their rifles, reassuring them, and doing everything to get them to the end of the march. In the midst of a violent shower we started to camp in a wood, moving in by platoons. The major had lost his way and had evidently decided to bunk up for the night. Before all the men got into the woods, where we could hear the sick fellows talking and crying out, orders came to move out again. So I had to pull the poor chaps out into the field where they sat down in lines in a resigned kind of way. The colonel had come to lead us to our billet. I could dimly make out his car down at the end of the field near the road, and there was a group of officers standing about waiting until the battalion could be hauled out of the woods again.

Once get four or five hundred dead tired men into a patch of thick, brambly, rain-soaked woods, and getting them out is no light task.

While our men were waiting I got permission from the colonel for them to smoke. It was really touching to see how hungry they were for tobacco. I never realized how much it could mean. I lit a cigarette myself, and remember it was more like eating something than smoking. The effect was so distinct as to be felt in the pit of the stomach. After a few puffs one felt the cold and damp less. Tobacco in times of great fatigue, annoyance, and nervous stress brings a slightly sleepy feeling of contentment and does not seem to lower the faculties much. It enables one to endure more.

After about an hour we marched, just a mile or so, and came to an immense grange; this was a French farm—barn, house, lofts, and everything—built in a great hollow square about a court and big enough in this case to billet the whole battalion.

We moved the men into various lofts filled with straw, while I found a large room downstairs where there were piles and piles of feather mattresses with a few French soldiers on them.

The French had been using this farm as a billet for some time, and a few of them were there when we arrived. I picked some of these mattresses out, told some of my friends about them, and after getting some scrambled eggs, new milk, and a pull of cognac in the kitchen (so much for speaking French), I turned in on a feather bed, after locking the door to keep all others out, and slept as I had never slept before. I was done—at the end. One slept so deeply as to lose any idea of the lapse of time.

Next morning the colonel came around raising Cain about our not attending to the gas cases. I turned over and let the captain take the hell. He was drawing the salary and the lieutenants had been doing the work lately. I think the shot told, as from then on he braced up and helped us out at every turn.

After breakfast a hint came around that we were to make an attack that night, so it would be a good thing to get reorganized.

Lieutenant Glendenning and I got the company together and called the roll, checking every one off carefully. We had lost so many that it was found possible to make only three platoons. We felt it was better to have three fairly strong platoons in the outfit than four weak ones. I purposely told the men what they were up against. A few of them later dropped out and went to hospital. Some of these, of course, were "gold-brickers" and some were really in bad shape. I cursed out the former, put them on a truck, and gave them my "blessing." As one of the sergeants remarked, "No half-baked birds in a battle for mine." What we had left were starved, hard and lean, and anxious to get a "swat" at "Fritz," after being pounded so unmercifully by his artillery. We were down to about 140 out of the 270 in the company* that had left New York—"attrition." After about half an hour's work picking the personnel for the new platoons, everything was ready for the move. We also took this occasion to sort and distribute the equipment as equably as possible. Then I went back and lay down again.

There was an old piano in the room with the feather beds, and some fool came in and played a lot of homesick airs. Everybody got that "Just Before the Battle, Mother" feeling. I nearly wilted myself, to tell the truth. Very often before we went out for some attack or other, one got that way. The feeling of utter yearning and despair, the fear of the last indignities ahead, and the knowledge that the war might go on for years and years, brought mental and physical paralysis to the individual. It is only the great machine of the army that then lays its iron touch on mind and body and makes it possible to go on—or it is a sense of responsibility. I know this is so, for men have told me, and I have seen and felt it.

* Owing to various causes this company had more than the usual quota.

Toward the Flame

I stopped the pianist. Under the spell of music the longing for persons one loves becomes so physical and acute that it makes a man ill. At Langres I went to a concert one afternoon, and certain melodies and rhythms, very strong in memories and suggestion, made me sweat as on a hot day, and finally, violently dizzy and sick. There was a French officer standing near who knew what was the matter, too. They had been at war so long in France, they understood.

At noon we marched, and a very historic march it was. We moved out onto a flat plateau and then stopped as they were shelling the road ahead. Once we got the order "To the rear" and then went on again. All the men laughed—some of the staff were getting close to the shells for the first time, it was rumored. The mules and horses got in great confusion at "To the rear," some turning right and some left, and stepping over the traces. But we finally got straightened out and on our way.

A German "sausage balloon" could be seen miles away. It must have been across the Marne. Once with a great buzzing and whirr two enemy planes sailed over us, coming up suddenly, looming black and large over the woods. There were orders here against firing at them in order to avoid being bombed. We got a gas alarm and walked needlessly for a mile or so with our masks on. Then they were taken off, and we began to go down into the wide valley of the Marne.

The March to Château-Thierry

The road was pitted on both sides and repaired from recent shell craters. We passed through a considerable town all riddled, with a barricade at one end, and camouflage over the road that made one think of the whipcord signals over railroad tracks just before a bridge or tunnel, but these were made of painted canvas stretched on wire. There was a brushwood screen for several miles going down the hill here on one side of the road. The overhead camouflage kept aviators from seeing down it for any great stretch. The country here was very sunny but deserted and still, crops standing in the fields. There was no firing to be heard.

A lot of French wagons and cavalry passed us going fast, and at last we came down a long hill, single file, into full view of the Marne and Château-Thierry, beautiful in the distance, and by that time in our hands.

It was the first time we really knew of the great withdrawal. The Germans had left the day before, and we had the railroad working already. It was a great pleasure to see engines again. They belonged to a comfortable world.

Toward the Flame

After waiting on the bridge that crossed the railroad near a big factory, the roof of which was literally riddled with shrapnel and bullets, we began to enter the town. It was fine to be in a city again, even a deserted one. Château-Thierry was beautiful even in its ruins. All the houses were looted as usual, but the place was not so badly shelled as most small villages we saw. The artillery had made some effort to save it, it seems.

We passed the colonel in his car before a temporary headquarters, and marched up the broad, branch-strewn street. At a turn we saw the town hall with a beautiful formal garden down a court, and a gilded clock tower with a big arch underneath. There were white statues, but the usual shell-holes were plentiful, of course. The streets were very wide, and the houses of nice architectural quality; some of them very fine, white, clean and handsome. The "All Highest" had been there June 2nd, and there were all kinds of evidences of German occupation. Most of the dead had been buried. Then we turned the corner suddenly and come out on the Marne.

I shall never forget that scene. It was late afternoon, the sun just sinking toward a hill, casting long shadows, and the river, which here made several turns, was very blue, running between the white desolate houses of the town like a stream through a cemetery. Farther down the Marne there was a vista of red-tiled roofs, and a wonderful Gothic church tower almost lacelike in its grace. A pair of stone water-horses were rearing under the stone bridge, which was cut in two by shells, but downstream there was a pontoon bridge, across which the army was moving in single file like ants over a bare, sunny place. Little groups of Frenchmen clad in blue were standing around, and as we got nearer there was a general air of gaiety discovered; some one was playing a march on a mouth organ, one of those gay, lilting French tunes. With the green grass, bright sun, and the deep, blue river it was almost pastoral, except for the endless line of men who walked across the pontoons, rifles slung. There was a dull shuffling sound and a clatter of boards as we crossed the floating bridge. One Frenchman caused not a little confusion by trying to cross with a bicycle—characteristically, trying to come the "wrong way." But this was soon stopped, and I crossed over and waited until the rear of the company came by, talking to some of the *poilus* on the bank in the meantime. There was a spirit of rejoicing in the air, a consciousness that the German tide was on the ebb. *"Américains et français, bons camarades,"* said one little soldier. I gave him a cigarette. At last the rear of the company passed with Lieutenant Glendenning cheering some of the weary along while carrying one old man's rifle. I got things straightened out a bit, and urged on the men who were lagging. "Only half a mile more"— a rough joke or two—and we went on.

Toward the Flame

The Germans were going, and going fast. So orders came to halt at Château-Thierry. We went up into a little suburb, a town called Brasles, along a valley with a mill stream, and camped there in the old houses. Some dug in. There were huge hills on either side—"204" was just across the valley—hills that had cost thousands of lives. The valley was full of immense shell craters full of water, and their great brown scars could be seen upon the hillsides. I found a place for my tent in a mint patch which rather mitigated a dead cow up the stream.

The houses were intensely interesting; full of all kinds of things one would have liked to carry off, and lots of "Boche stuff," too. They had got out in a dreadful hurry. The little suburb must have been delightful in peace: a lovely old church, charming houses, an old mill, a priest's house, and a beautiful view,—very much like the scenes on teacups.

We were all tickled to death at not having to go into a battle that night. There was nothing to eat, however, that is, no hot meal. Our kitchens had to wait until the big bridge was repaired. I ate some chocolate, and then just about the time we were settled, an order came from the major to establish an outpost.

This order was more or less of a formality as we had no contact with the enemy, but Lieutenant Glendenning and I went up on a high hill behind Château-Thierry, overlooking the camp, in order to place our outposts where they could see over the next ridge. The hillside had a lot of abandoned German batteries on it. Here the effect of our big guns, the ones we had heard at Nogent, was apparent, for the Germans had been blown off the hill, literally. One cleverly hidden battery after another had been wrecked. One dugout in a granite pile had been safe, and there was a wrecked farmhouse near by which we entered to investigate.

As we got close three Germans slunk into the woods. It was getting twilight and we felt rather uneasy, not knowing how many there might be about. Glen and I had left our pistols behind, and I had no helmet. We whistled up the rest of the patrol pretty lively, spread out in fan shape, and came in on the house from all directions—no one!

A couple of minutes later a sergeant with another American patrol came up. I knew by his use of the third person in addressing me that he was a regular. "Does the lieutenant desire," etc. It sounded very Chinese at the front. He turned out to be from the 4th U. S. Infantry. Francis Hogan, a friend of mine, was in that regiment, and I determined to see him that night. It was one of those decisions that comes of itself and leaves no doubt in your mind that it is what you are going to do.

The boys from the 4th had had nothing to eat for some time, so we went down to find what they might have at brigade headquarters and to report to Gen-

eral Weigel that we were in touch with the 4th Infantry. The general came out, much pleased to get
the information, and by a little verbal maneuvering
I got direct orders to complete *liaison,* find out where
the front line was, and carry a message to the colonel
of the 4th Infantry. The less men I had, the quicker
going, I thought. So I borrowed Sergeant Davidson's pistol and set out with Lieutenant Glendenning
to find the 4th Infantry all by ourselves. Our way
led directly through the forest.

The other regiment of our brigade was just coming
into camp and hindered us until we left them behind,
putting up their pup tents in the little wooded valley
in the rear of the town. We then followed a well-

marked road that led into the
woods, and we walked and walked.
I had questioned the sergeant of
the 4th and at first had some idea
of our direction. But after a while
it began to dawn on us that we
were getting into "No Man's
land."

German shells lay everywhere
in wicker baskets; we tripped over
old telephone wires; and now and
then there was a dead man lying
here and there at the edge of the
thickets. There was a good deal of
mustard gas about, too, our own,

which we had thrown at the enemy, so at times we had to wear our masks. Ahead of us there was a great red light in the sky. I thought it was a burning town. We passed across roads with German sign-boards, *"Ludendorff Strasse,"* and such names. I once talked over turning back with Glen, but we were so far already that we both determined to go ahead. We tramped on and on.

Quite suddenly we came out onto a great wheat field, with mist in the hollow places. They looked like lakes in the moonlight. About a mile or so away was the front line; big red flares going up (my burning town), "whizzbangs," and machine guns going every now and then. We skirted along in the shadow of the woods, and just where a promontory of trees ran out into the field I saw a group of men. They saw us, too! I watched their flankers go out with the cold bayonets—there was nothing to be done—so we walked over toward them. If they were Germans, we had met the enemy and we were theirs. "Halt, youse guys," said an Irish voice. It was a platoon of the 4th Infantry which like us had just worked up through the woods.

I explained my mission to the lieutenant in charge and both of us showed him our identification cards. There were too many English-speaking Germans about just then to take chances. Another platoon emerged about this time and told us where the 4th was. I also got a little idea how the war was being fought. No one knew for certain who was on either flank, in front or behind. It seems the French were actually on the line that night just a few thousand yards ahead.

I swallowed a whole mouthful of gas and pride to think that Glen and I were probably the only two lieutenants in the whole division who really knew the exact location and status of things at that time. This gave me a curious insight, and I heard, when I got back, certain officers, supposed to be tactical wizards, holding forth on absolutely wrong premises. The

only way is to run along and see for yourself. It is a fine little habit.

I wish I could picture accurately the plateau above Château-Thierry that night: the white, misty moonlight, the sense of dread and mystery in the black masses of woods ahead with the enemy's stars and rockets curving over them, only to glimmer away; the sullen glow of the giant red flare, the far-off thunder toward Rheims, and the crimson splashes in the sky. Across the liquid grain fields lay white tomb-like villages loud with the sudden chatter or thumping of machine guns that would suddenly subside, leaving a few strange cries floating over the dark figures of our own men, or the wind rippling the lake-like wheat,—then the stars, and all-engulfing silence.

About this time a French officer met us and told us the 89th French Division was hustling "Fritz" along. Fritz was still going east and now and then celebrated his departure with a lot of fireworks. A regular Chinese New Year's broke out in a little town up the road, where the French were moving in. I soon got word that there was a major near by commanding a battalion of the 4th Infantry who could tell me where his regimental command post was located, so we started back.

After skirting along an old German trench, and getting on a blind track once, we met another platoon of the 4th with German prisoners. The woods still had quite a number of stragglers in them. Glen and I must have looked fine coming through all alone with one pistol—dog luck!

At last we found the major of the 4th with a machine gun company all lined up along the side of the hill just like a cut in the tactics book. They had halted and were waiting for news from ahead. We walked out of the mist onto these men, and I was taken to the major.

He was glad to hear what I knew, and told me he was out of touch with his colonel who was at a little place called Gland farther down the valley. I got the general direction of the town, after which Glen and I took off down the hill, through some quarries, and hit a road that led us into Gland, a small village terribly wrecked. In the moonlight it reminded me of some of the flat-roofed towns along the Mexican border.

The colonel of the 4th Infantry had his command post under the church in a deep vault. One entered through a dark passageway from which every gleam of light was carefully excluded, and then suddenly came into the groined arches under the church, lit with a mellow glow of candles, and very quiet on account of the telephone, although full of men. The voice of an interpreter examining a German prisoner by the colonel's table at the other end of the room sounded harsh and grating. There were a good many American officers standing about. The orderlies and runners with their red armbands were sleeping or sitting back in the farther recesses under the arches. In the full light, by a map on the table, sat the French *liaison* officer, conspicuous in his gold and blue.

I delivered General Weigel's message to the colonel, and told him the disposition of his own men of the 4th that we had seen coming through the woods. My message was simply the information that our own brigade was in support at Brasles. The colonel questioned me closely, filling in on a map now and then data which were evidently not complete. Then he delivered a little homily to me and Glen on the subject of wandering around the front without helmets, and gave me, through one of his officers, the exact situation of the enemy and of our own troops that night. The Germans were retreating, but were still holding villages farther up the valley by rear guard actions. The 4th certainly had their *liaison* and general map information well in hand just then.

I told the colonel that I wanted to see a friend in "M" company of his regiment, so he gave me a sergeant major as guide. It turned out that Francis Hogan's company was quartered just across the street—if quartered you could call it.

On the other side of the street was a high, white stone wall over which we could see the second story of a large, ruined house against the sky. After some parley at the gate as to the location of my friend's platoon, we entered and found ourselves in a garden strewn with wreckage, with the big, blank walls of the house looming above us and the stars shining faintly through the gaping windows and shell-holes. The men were sleeping all over the place, wrapped close in their ghostly slickers. With the pale, glimmering walls and white stones scattered about by the bombardment, it was like a cemetery. We found my friend's lieutenant and wakened him. He was very courteous although very tired, and, calling the sergeant on duty, told him to find Corporal Hogan.

We went around waking the men, apparently an endless task. Some pretended to be asleep, thinking a detail was being called. I worked in great haste, with Glen helping me, as it was getting along toward morning.

It seemed for a while that after coming all that way I was not to find Frank. Then suddenly we came across him sleeping by a great, white stone. He sprang up as men do at the front on being awakened, but he knew me instantly. He was looking thin, but straight and wiry and hard. We peered into each other's faces in the dark and sat down on the stone together and had a close talk. He spoke of letters he had written me that I had never received and gave me the address of a friend, Dabney Frazier, in the Marines, whom we had both known in happy times. I did not tell him that I knew this lad had been killed. We seemed too close to it all then.

While we were still talking they began to shell. The shells passed so close over the garden that we could feel their wind. They lit along the road beyond with a glare and a smash which compelled us to fall each time by instinct. It was impossible to talk any longer. We promised to try to see each other at every opportunity. Glen and I stood up between shells to make a run for it. I remember I had an impulse to take Frank with me, but I only shook hands with him. As we said good-bye, he thrust a letter into my hands. I never saw him again. He was a brilliant and promising poet. He was killed in the Argonne in October a few days before the armistice.

Glen and I timed the shells—every three minutes. We ran for it, and ducked into the road ditch every time one came. Luckily, they were passing over the road by this time and falling into a swamp. Each one spattered us with mud, but there were no solid fragments. As we ran madly down the highway, we passed a company cooker with its fire going, and backed up against the bank with two quivering horses. The cook had thoughtfully betaken himself to parts unknown.

Glen and I snatched a cup of coffee and ran for it again. The last shell nearly got us, but we got through into Brasles. "Jerry" had skipped them right down the road after us. It seemed as though he knew he was gunning for us. I met Orville Thompson, an old home town boy, and captain of Company "M," standing in the doorway of the village. It was his company cooker that we had passed, and he was watching the result of the shelling rather anxiously. One hates to lose one's kitchen.

Another half hour and we were back again at brigade headquarters. We found the general and his adjutant sleeping in their automobile, and reported the situation to them. The general was much pleased to get the information. Then we went back to our own colonel, wakened him in an old cellar, and told him; after that, "home" to a ruined billet. By the light of the setting moon some of our regiment's cookers were coming up the white roads, smoking and smelling deliciously of coffee. We found Nick had something hot for us, and a bed on a mattress in the cellar of the priest's house, safe from any possible shells. After such a tremendous night and day, both of us turned in and slept like the dead on the fields outside.

CHAPTER V

A DAY AT CHÂTEAU-THIERRY

FORTUNATELY, the day after we returned from our reconnaissance, the brigade did not move, but lay all day and well up into the next night at Château-Thierry and in the little suburb of Brasles. Glen and I slept long into the morning, and were only wakened at last by faithful Nick coming into our cellar with some steaming mess pans full of oatmeal, and, wonderful to say, milk and sugar.

The mess sergeant had been lucky in finding a

commissary where he could get some "tin cow," always a delicacy at the front.

The mattresses, which the Germans had taken from some French bedroom, were luxurious. I can remember yet lying in that damp, moldy-smelling cellar and looking out at the bright sunlight and green grass framed by the door where some one passed now and then. What a luxury, a real bed! To my dying day the damp odor of mold will always bring to mind some dark hole of a dugout or a cellar filled with old mattresses, but cool and restful, dark and safe.

After a while Glen and I stretched, put on our puttees and shoes, and went out. One never undressed at the front. Of course, I felt especially dirty and dusty from the trip of the night before, and so began to speculate on clean clothes and a bath. So far I had been lucky in having only a few weeks between sanitary opportunities.

The men were moving about over the little suburb. Most of the small jobs of the morning were finished by now, and, as the halt was obviously meant for a rest, everybody was taking advantage of it.

Nick and I explored the priest's house in the cellar of which we had been staying. It was full of pitiful reminders of the parish life. He must have been rather a pleasant man I imagine, that priest. There were little picture cards scattered everywhere: small Bible scenes that took me back with a leap to my own little Sunday school class as a lad—Jesus in a red coat, surrounded by lambs, the Virgin, tinsel hearts, and prayer books. One of those Nick took and kept with a simple Catholic faith that I envied at that time.

Upstairs, in a wash stand, was a box with some old coins, overlooked by the Germans by some miracle. The priest had evidently collected them from time to time. There was one with the prominent-nosed profile of Louis XVI on it and the legend, *"Le Roi, la Loi, la Foi,"* by which I judged it to be of a very early revolutionary issue. There were also one or two medallions: a swimming medal issued by some French city to commemorate a long-forgotten event, and several other old and curious ones. These I lost later on, as one lost everything, from baggage to life, somewhere between the Marne and the Vesle.

One's chief impression of these looted houses was the litter of plaster, glass, and tramped articles on the floor. The heavy hobnail shoes ground everything to powder and came out slightly whitened from the dust after each trip. It was not hard to tell where a man had been. All you had to do was to look at his shoes.

Downstairs, next door, there had been a carpenter's or woodcarver's shop. Here the German soldiers had evidently been amusing themselves with the Frenchman's tools, for a number of our men had little carved wood figures that they had found and were keeping as souvenirs, all rather well done, but unmistakably Teutonic.

There is a peculiar quality about all things German, a certain aspect, something in the very grin of the carved cupids on their inkstands, that seems to cry aloud, "We do not come from Rome, and Greece is not our home." That was the way those little manikins impressed me.

The men were tramping around through the houses, and there seemed to be a general flow down the road toward the Marne. As those coming back reported the presence of both a Y.M.C.A. canteen and a quartermaster distributing new clothes, I betook myself in that general direction.

In the valley the gigantic shell craters were as full of rusty water as ever. And I noticed, as I passed over the creek, which ran with a big volume of water, that the smell of something dead was tremendous, probably an old cow, whose bloated carcass lay half concealed somewhere up the stream. Despite all that, the spot was beautiful.

From a little footbridge one could look back and see the line of white houses meeting the intense green of the grass, with here and there a cooker smoking under a shed. Along the road going up the valley, a crowd was gathering to watch some prisoners that were being marched down. Groups of our men were sitting in the vacant windows, and for the first time in many days, there seemed to be a feeling of relaxation in the air. The battle for the time being had gone on.

I continued down the valley, meeting more and more men, till I suddenly came out on the main road where there was a great crowd gathered around a number of trucks.

I pressed my way through, exchanging a few greetings with officers, and friends among the men, and after some little hustling, found myself gazing up at a couple of very busy and harassed-looking men on the Y.M.C.A. truck, who were engaged in answering the same questions a million times while trying to make change—an impossible task with the French money. They were selling tobacco, confections, and toilet articles. The end-gate of the truck was down, and over this was passed the merchandise which had been piled up at the other end of the truck ready for sale. I was unable to get any chocolate.

"Out of chocolate," the Y.M.C.A. "bird" said a thousand times; so I made him say it for me, and got some razor blades, a few cakes, and cigarettes instead, afterward strolling over to the quartermaster's trucks that were purring away by the roadside in the midst of 500 men, naked, and in all stages of undress. The quartermaster was issuing new clothes.

You walked up to a truck, and after waiting your turn, got as near the proper size of clothing as possible. You then went aside, picked a comfortable spot somewhere, and changed clothes, throwing the old dirty clothes on the respective pile for each article. There were little mountains of shirts, coats, underwear, and shoes, salvage piles which later on would be taken behind the lines to be cleaned and renovated. I got a new outfit from head to foot, uniform and all. By that time many of the officers had discarded leather puttees and insignia. I was one of those who aped the humble private most closely— and a very wise thing it was to do.

Having clean socks and underwear and a tight-fitting new uniform was a pleasant sensation that needed only a bath to make it complete. The sight of the Marne, about a quarter of a mile away, glancing merrily in the sun, made a suggestion too strong to resist.

On my way down to the river I ran into the headquarters company and picked up Lieutenant "Bill" Snow, who was having a vehement argument with his captain about the mess. The one pound cannon platoon wasn't getting fed, or its share, or something, or so I gathered. He got a towel, however, and joined me. "Bill" was lately from Virginia and knew how to enjoy life. The mess question could be argued again. On the way down to the river the French *liaison* officer with the regiment joined us with one or two others.

Between Château-Thierry and the Marne there is a flat that cost many lives to take. We came out on this wide, grassy meadow from a little garden, where there was a pear tree with a big, broken, white, splintered limb near a shell-hole, and walked over to the river, a gay enough little group, some of the luckier ones with towels over their arms.

Near the river bank in a little screen of willows was a pit sunk in the red earth where a German machine gun nest had been. The feet of a dead man stuck out from the bushes near by, and there was the usual litter of used shells and broken stuff about. Evidently they had got him by artillery, for there were lots of rather small shell-holes about. One could imagine him waiting there, hoping against hope, until that last one came. He looked to be about 35 years old. "We shall all be changed . . . in the twinkling of an eye," says the apostle. In war-time the real meanings of old sayings revive with new force. They were written in times when life and death were not mere amenities.

Bathing was not so easy as we had imagined. There was a rather steep little bank at the edge of the water, about a four-foot drop, and then a ledge of very sticky, white clay. We threw our clothes on the grass and finally worked our way in, large gobs of the putty-like material adhering to the humbler portions of our frames. The water was cold and very clear and blue. Once in, it was glorious. What a sparkle and warmth to the sun! I could see almost as far as Nogent. About 100 yards downstream one of our men and a *poilu* were "fishing" by throwing hand grenades into the Marne. The wisdom of eating fish at this time was doubtful; the river must have been full of dead Germans, and the conclusion, at least for me, was obvious.

The French *liaison* officer was a fine swimmer and had a ghastly scar where his shoulder had been blown loose at the siege of Verdun. It had kept him, he said, nine months in the hospital; but here he was, a gay, strong, and rather handsome fellow, swinging his heels carelessly on the muddy bank and giving vent to his French wit in newly acquired and profane Americanisms. A fine example of "decadent" France.

After the usual trouble in scraping off the mud, we returned to the town where there was the customary rumor of a move going about. I left Bill Snow renewing his argument with his captain, just where it had been left off. There was nothing else for him to do. I, for my part, reported back to my company.

Supper was under way, but a very slim one I was told. However, for some that was just as well. Under the mill wheel just where we had been camping, the men found a dead German floating in a covered part of the mill race. This accounted for the uncommon strength of the atmosphere in the vicinity. We had really overrated the dead cow. The German was swollen to an immense size. Only his belt seemed to hold him together, and we disposed of him in a good old Biblical fashion by hanging a millstone around his neck and sinking him. If the owner of that mill ever reads this, he will be satisfied, as a good Frenchman, I am sure, to know to what use his nether millstone was put.

Rumor for once was right. About five o'clock the order came from headquarters to move, and the mess lines were hurried somewhat in order to get the rolling kitchens in shape for the expected night's march. This happened again and again. A great many times the men were cut off from being served, in the middle of a mess line, or had hastily to bolt their food in order to appease a worried company commander who was afraid that the order to march would find his outfit in the midst of a meal. Mess gear would be hastily cleared up, scrubbed out with a piece of paper and some sand or earth, after which the usual delay of several hours ensued. It seemed to be true, though, that if we resumed the serving of the meal, the order to march was sure to catch us in the middle of the operation. "Play safe," is written on the hearts of all captains, so we played safe—and hungry.

We moved out that night suspiciously promptly, the major and his staff riding and bobbing on ahead, as usual, up the little valley that led away from Château-Thierry. They were followed by the streaming column of men with packs, and rifles carried at all angles. We were down in a deep rut of a vale with immense hills on all sides, the famous "204" toward Vaux rising to the left, and a high hill with the little town of Gland on the other side, to the right, where I had found my friend the night before. Back of us lay the white city with blank staring windows and ruined church towers; on either side and in front, dense woods with an air of twilight mystery over all, a tender summer evening along the grassy Marne.

We marched a little while and then stopped, falling out along the road where another regiment of the brigade was lined up ready to move after we should pass them. The colonel of that command and his staff came down the hillside out of one of the dugouts near the gigantic shell-holes. I saw the old deserted farmhouse where the Germans had sneaked away only the night before. It looked more ghostly and deserted than ever. Presently some of the officers wandered up and we began to have a little chat.

Every halt was the signal for the "rag chewers" to gather. We were all much exercised in our battalion that we were short of provisions which had not caught us up, because the bridge over the Marne had not been repaired yet. Bill Snow boasted that he got his one-pounders over it by the old dodge of not understanding the protests of the French, and apologizing after his guns were on the right side. He had dragged them over the footbridge. There were some fine rumors passed around as to hearing something the colonel let drop about appointing so-and-so captain, and then a general growl at the policy of getting rid of certain officers, not personally on the right side of the powers, by sending them home to train troops instead of sending *us,* "the hard workers."

How we all hoped that we should be sent home! Promotion, and nothing to worry about, a reprieve from the imminence of death. All this was cut short by the order to move on.

It took a long while to get started with the large intervals between the platoons and companies, so necessary in case a shell came.

We marched that night for several miles. It always seemed as if no one knew where we were going, and very often they didn't. Perhaps to a vague name on the map. Up the same roads and through the same woods that Glen and I had traversed the night before, we moved through the same mysterious jumble of crossroads, German telephone lines, signs, piles of ammunition, and the faint ghastly smell of mustard gas to depress us. It was growing dark now, and a storm seemed to be coming on. One wondered how and where the night was to be spent. We were only too soon to find out.

In a sort of amphitheater in the hills we halted near a crossroads. The road at right angles to ours came down a hill and then shot up through the woods on the other side like a sword-cut through the forest. It seemed like the prism of a canal through the wall of trees, and it disappeared mysteriously over the crest of the hill into the beyond. Once in a while there was the faint, restless flicker of artillery somewhere on the other side of the Marne, and now and then a shell fell in the forest far away, but just near enough to make one wonder a little—trust "Fritz" for that. Our battalion turned off on the side road, and the orders were to put the men in the woods for the night.

Followed the usual hunt to find a place to conceal the kitchen and horses. We found a good shelter, but it was in the woods on the other side of a rather bad ditch along the road. The platoons turned into the woods with the usual grumbling. The men could not understand why they had left comfortable billets in Brasles to march out a few miles to camp in the woods. Going to bed in a gas-smelling thicket is not much fun. I heard the usual cracking of sticks, swearing, driving of tent pegs; one or two of the sergeants came out and reported that moving about so much was kicking up a good deal of gas, and the men were getting nervous about it. One of the hardest things an officer has to do is to enforce a stupid order when the men are intelligent enough to know better. That is where "discipline" generally and fortunately breaks down in the American army. On the other side of the road was an open field free from gas.

Cries of "gas" began to go up on all sides. Pretty soon some one in the valley, after one of the far-away shells lit, gave the alarm by firing off a pistol or gun. The alarm spread like wildfire, and this time I learned what *wildfire* meant. From every woods and grove around all that amphitheater of hills came a surge of red spots and dots that marked the discharge of rifles and pistols fired into the air; cries of "gas" and a crackle of musketry sounded like a stage battle. The effect was almost grand. It was also grimly amusing and annoying.

To those who have never experienced the nerve strain at the front, the psychology of such a false alarm can scarcely be understood. The men had been taught to put the gas mask on and to give the alarm at the slightest indication or sniff. This, of course, was nonsense, as around the front one came into contact with and breathed more or less gas of one kind or another half the time, especially in the woods.* Given a condition such as existed, however, with the men trained to believe that a light sniff might mean death, with nerves highly strung by being shelled more or less for a month or so, and the presence of not a few who really had been gassed,— it is no wonder that a gas alarm went beyond all bounds. It was remarked as a joke that when some one yelled, "Gas!" everybody in France put on the mask. At any rate, the alarm often spread for miles.

For instance, a stray shell would fall into or near some group or outfit at night, and the alarm would be given; automobile horns would be honked, empty

* The men had been trained for gas conditions in trench warfare.

brass shells beaten, rifles emptied, and the mad cry would be taken up and passed on over hill and vale till it sounded like the Chinese trying to chase off an eclipse. For miles around, scared soldiers woke up in the midst of the frightful pandemonium and donned their gas masks, only to hear a few minutes later the cry, "All safe,"—then they would take them off again amid laughter and oaths. Two or three such alarms a night were frequent. "Gas shock" was really as frequent as shell shock.

It was such an alarm as this that had started in the little amphitheater of hills where we were about to bivouac. In a few minutes all the good of the rest we had had at Brasle passed away. The men in the woods thrashed around and did stir up some gas, and as the large number of gas cases which our company had suffered in "Death Valley" had made "B" company very leery, there ensued one of the worst nights I ever spent.

Numbers of the non-commissioned officers came out on the road to tell me that the woods where the platoons were lying were full of "mustard." They begged me to move the company out of the thicket. One Italian sergeant, an excellent scout and rifleman, but rather flighty, became hysterical, and several others followed. This man really had been slightly gassed before, and the smell of it among the leaves drove him frantic. It took several men to hold him down, and I had to bring him out onto the road. Calls and cries came from the woods from all directions, so finally the battalion gas officer arrived to ascertain the state of affairs. He had just come back from a British "gas school," and was so full of chemical formulas that he couldn't apprehend the fact that we were suffering from the fear of gas rather than from the gas itself. It took a good deal of bluster on my part to get him to allow me to move the men into the ditch beside the road. As it was perfectly dark, there could have been no objection to it, provided we went back into cover at dawn. Pretty soon I had runners out to each platoon and the dark bodies of men could be seen sleeping along the ditch. A few of the more nervous ones began digging in. The next thing was to get the cooker up the hill.

We hitched all four horses taken from both the cooker and the carts to the kitchen, and then got them on the run. With much swearing and cracking of whips the big rolling steamer came up the hill, striking sparks from the stones, and coming to a violent halt opposite the place we had chosen for it. Then it was backed into the woods by main force and over the ditch amid a great scrambling of horses' hoofs and the grunts and efforts of a black mass of men striving against the wheels and spokes with tense arms and shoulders. What a relief, when the horses were tethered at last and the comfortable crunching in the nose bags began, and the men had gone back to sleep! After that it started to drizzle, so the whole company had to be wakened again one by one to put on slickers. I mention all these things just to show what it meant even to make a halt.

I shall never forget that night. I crawled under the cooker, still a little warm, to get out of the drizzle, and slept profoundly. It was like dying for an hour or two. Then I woke up suddenly. One of the horses was very near and the forest was dripping. I walked out into the road, rather stiff, and started to pace up and down the hill where the men were sleeping. In the faint glimmer I could make out the gray forms in the just visible slickers along the road ditch. They were sleeping like the dead, literally.

The faces of a sleeping army are wonderful. All the lines are relaxed, all the pettinesses, weaknesses, vices, stand out. The weak jaws and chins fall open and droop, the lines on both sides of the nose grow deeper—only on a few, mostly the very young—there comes a calm and a sweetness, a light grace in the sleeping attitude that justifies the worship of youth. Now and then a horse stamped with a faint jingle of harness, and down at the crossroads once or twice a side car chugged by. Something in the air began to hint of morning, and the usual artillery barrage was getting under way.

It was the insistence of the artillery that made me suspect that we were soon to take part in a big move. All the forest began to tremble with the sound of the huge guns, many of them miles away across the

A Day at Château-Thierry

Marne. The sky wavered and slobbered bestially with red. Towards the north, across a crest that stood out dimly against the sky, there was the infernal, scarlet glow that told where the big game was on. Pretty soon a runner came to summon me to battalion headquarters, so I wakened the first sergeant and told him to have the men ready to move when I came back. I knew in my bones we must move soon.

The major had his headquarters—the word might be in quotation marks—by the crossroads at the bottom of the hill. It consisted of a pup tent stretched over some branches, and a hole in the ground in which he was sitting like a man in a bathtub. The adjutant was holding a lantern over some maps and trying to shade it carefully at the same time. A group of company commanders and officers were sprawled about in all attitudes, trying to crawl into the tent to get a look at the map and to hear the orders which the major was reading. Some one at the crossroads was calling, "Put out that light," while the major was insisting that it be kept lit in order to read his orders which in the dark would be manifestly impossible. All this, of course, kept the adjutant in a great sweat, as there was an iron-clad order not to show lights of any kind. Finally, we came to understand that we were to move immediately.

The captain, who had been with the major most

of the night, went back with me to the company, which was already lined up on the road. In a few minutes, we were moving down the hill. It was Company "B's" turn to lead.* We moved only as far as the crossroads, however, and then halted again in order to allow the other two battalions that were coming up the road to pass us at the corners. The colonel drove up in his car, and the staffs of the different battalions gathered around him.

At the crossroads there was a sort of circular clearing in the woods, and here, while our men sat down, I watched the other two battalions of the regiment go by. With the colonel there, it seemed almost like a review. They turned the corner and passed up the

road, each company halting to allow the one ahead to gain distance—then straight up the steep hill where the road made its knife-like cut through the forest. It seemed a perpendicular hill, with a gray streak of dawn at the top, and a strange abandoned enemy observation tower, camouflaged with leaves, rising out of the woods against the sky. The brown

* The various companies in a battalion took their respective turns in the order of march from day to day, as did the battalions in a regiment, etc., etc.

oblongs of men in column of squads crawled up it and disappeared.

While we watched there the dull gray east kept getting lighter, and the cannonade, the fierce roaring, barking sound of the barrage, grew till it was a vast earth-shaking roar, a deep, vibrant thunder; the red splashes of the guns breaking up out of the forest at acute angles where here and there a new battery went into action. Company after company reached the corner, halted, and then went on. I was greatly impressed that morning by the men.

It was the first time that I had seen the entire regiment since we had been in action. Most of the men who were passing by were by that time the "veterans" of several battles. Some had been at Hill Two Hundred and Four, some near Vaux in the trenches, and some in the Marne Valley and at Cemetery Hill when the Germans came across the Marne on pontoon bridges one fateful July morning. They looked seasoned, weighed, and not found wanting. The equipment they carried told the tale. The little funnel-mouthed *Chauchats,** the round ammunition panniers for magazines, the bombs, the funnels for the rifle grenades, all proved that this was no peace-time review. But most significant of all were the set faces under the "tin hats."

During one of the halts in the passing column, Lieutenant Wyke came over and sat down beside me

* An automatic rifle of French design used by the American forces.

97

for a little talk. He had been sent by General Weigel a few days before to make a reconnaissance and a report on Hill Two Hundred and Four after the enemy had left it. Sitting there, he described it to me. It was the great hill near Château-Thierry, which had balked us so long, and cost so many good French and American lives to take.

Wyke began to dribble souvenirs from his pockets. There was a map of the defenses of the hill, which he had taken from a dead German officer, probably the one that Lieutenant Shenkel had shot. This map showed the zones of machine gun fire, and an arrangement of wooden machine guns in a copse that drew the fire of our men, while the real guns were actually situated over the crest of the hill and used indirect fire. Wyke had also found the bodies of the dead from the platoons of "A" and "B" companies that had made the attack on the hill mentioned sometime earlier. His was one of the most painful stories I ever listened to; we had both known the men intimately. They had remained unburied for about two weeks and lay just as they had fallen, some had evidently been trying to help a wounded comrade. One man, a fine young bank clerk, who had kept our company books for us beautifully at Camp Hancock, had been killed after being wounded. He first sat up to try and dress his own wounds. Others had been shredded by shrapnel beyond recognition, and all were in terrible condition. The flesh had adhered to the identification tags which were corroded white, and hard to read. They smelled dreadfully in the envelope in which my friend delivered them to me. The folly of thinking that all the dead of the A.E.F. could be brought home is too ghastly to be laughable, even in its extreme nonsense. Wyke had given all of these martyrs as decent a burial as he could. There was an affection and manliness about his story that, as I looked at him, made me hope with all my heart that he would get through.

He also told me about the Great German dugout at the back of Hill Two Hundred and Four, where the Germans had dragged the good things of Château-Thierry—books from La Fontaine's library, crystal chandeliers, wine and carpets. There were women's clothes there, too. Then as his company moved, we shook hands, and he went away.

In a few minutes our turn came, and we passed our fine colonel looking firm-lined, capable, and positive, yet kindly withal. I heard the cheery greeting of Captain Gill, the regimental adjutant,—and we were climbing the hill. The battle ahead was growing. There was an immense volume of sound that morning like the hurtling noise that precedes an express train. It was the drumfire of our barrage. By now it was quite light.

At the top of the hill we passed the German observation tower. Some of the observing instruments were still in it. With its leaf-covered porches and

tree ladders, it looked like a house the Swiss Family
Robinson might have built. There was a litter of
personal belongings about, and one or two dugouts
near.

We had reached the crest now and began to march
over a rolling plateau quite flat at first, through miles
of woods all bearing evidence of the recent enemy
occupation. Piles of shells lay every few hundred
yards in carefully woven, wicker receptacles; deserted chairs were scattered around through the
woods in friendly groups, gun pits, occasionally little
houses and arbors, with maybe a bureau or an odd
bit of furniture quite lonely—and always the little,
mound-like dugouts like a beaver colony, where the
batteries had been.

The march that morning was the worst we ever
made. Not that it was so long, but we had not eaten
much the night before. It had been a hard night and
a long wait, and it looked like a battle ahead. We
were on the east side of the river, headed north, and
as we rose higher and higher, we could look now and
then into the valley of the Marne. Once there was a
glimpse of the white town of Château-Thierry where
we had been the night before. How peaceful! Over
there, though, from the heights on the far side of the
Marne came the barrage that was passing over our
heads. They were blasting "Fritz" loose again.

CHAPTER VI

ON THE EDGE OF THE BATTLE

THAT a great battle was on just ahead of us became increasingly evident. Not only the sounds, but the sights along the roads bore witness to it. The fight had evidently passed that way just a few hours before. All the banks of the roads were pitted with little man-holes where our men had frantically dug themselves in. Now and then an exhausted man, probably a runner at his post, or some electrician, lay wrapped up in his blanket all curled into a hole in the clay road bank like a locust in a stump. The freshly laid telephone wires followed the road, leading on and on to the front. We passed a few wounded men coming back, too pale and tired to answer questions. Side cars drove past like a shot out of a gun. The poplar trees lining the roads were shivered and torn and their branches littered the ground.

After a while we passed one of those large brick farmhouses, an immense hollow square of brick buildings enclosing an inner court, so common to the country between the Marne and the Vesle. There had been a German headquarters here, but an American staff had now occupied it, and there was a stream of cars and trucks replenishing the nearby dumps, and messengers on motorcycles dashing back and forth. The place had been terribly shelled. Portions of the walls along the road were thrown down or had great holes let in them, through which we could look as through a window and see the garden inside. The trees there were torn apart as if a cyclone had passed, and the walls were chipped and pitted by machine gun fire. A medical unit had established a dressing station in a barn.

The wounded lay along the road in rows, some sitting, and many blood-soaked and unattended. Some were in a frightfully nervous state, shrieking when a battery of 75's fired, which it did every few minutes. The guns were set right out in the fields and along the road, with their trail pieces newly dug in.

On the Edge of the Battle

The noise was terrific, making us stagger as we passed. It was like being close to a blast when it unexpectedly goes off. They were shelling a wood directly opposite, so the pieces were laid almost level. Even in daylight there was a blinding glare like taking a flash-light photograph, then a blow of sound and air followed as if one were being shoved by a drunken man.

Backed into the ditch near one battery was a Ford ambulance which had been struck by shrapnel. The driver had been killed. He was sitting with his head resting on the wheel, his hands hanging down dripping blood. A wounded man on the upper row of stretchers was also dead. We could look in as we passed. The stiff angle of the feet was characteristic, and the dark purple stains of the blood on his khaki showed that he had been dead some time. Old blood stains look as though someone had wiped his hands on brown clothes after picking elderberries—dark and purple.

Fatigue was beginning to tell on us by this time. We had marched miles. It was over twelve hours since we had eaten, and then very little. You must imagine us moving along both sides of the road in single file with a couple of paces

103

between the men, rifles slung and heads hung low, every one trying to accomplish the next step with the least expenditure of energy possible.

Each platoon and company had considerable distance between them, and kept touch by a thin thread of connecting files. Thus the regiment was strung out for miles. From a little rise we could look back and see the officers on horseback standing out startlingly plain like cardboard miniatures. "Inch-high horses and pea-sized men." It looked as though a vast Indian tribe were on the move. Such a formation brought only a few men within the bursting radius of a shell, in case the road were shelled, and also allowed the traffic free way down the highways.

The captain became too exhausted to do anything but plod right ahead. The spectacle of this middle-aged man stumbling along towards battle, sick at heart for his family at home, and sick of body from an empty stomach, was one of the finest exhibitions of real patriotism that I ever saw. What a pity there was not some better use for it.

I walked up and down the line joking with the men. They were game; even the weaker boys smiled back at me, though too tired to move their jaws to say anything. A few clowns at a time like this are invaluable. One Pole we had enlisted began a Polish song about something in Polish. It was, in fact, absolutely Polish. Its rhythm and gibberish were irresistibly funny and helped out a weary half mile.

On the Edge of the Battle

Everything we wore began to trouble us. My pack made my shoulders ache intolerably. The pistol dragged down, rubbed my hip bone, and chafed a sore place on my leg. Places on my feet and legs began to smart. The outer world seemed to recede to a vast distance; the landscape took on an odd gray appearance. One became preoccupied with musing upon one's self.

Halts were the worst. After each one it was harder than ever to get the men on their feet. Some began to gag. Slightly gassed men showed symptoms of giving out, and the young boys seemed about to be toppled over backward by their packs when they got up. Nearly all the canteens were long ago dry.

At one halt Nick brought me a piece of bread and a drink of wine. He must have been saving it for the last. I ate it secretly to avoid the eyes of the men, sharing some of it with Glendenning who came up from the rear, evidently ghastly tired. He had been carrying some of the weaker lads' rifles and was loaded down. The wine and bread made a new world for both of us and enabled me to pull through. I must have walked a quarter again as much as the men, going up and down the line, and had to keep on my feet at halts to look after the sick. Some simple medicines I carried helped a growing nausea greatly.

We tackled another rise at last, which some of the men could never have made had it not been that word

came back we were near our halting place. The battle ahead had died down, news which, strange as it may seem, cheered me up greatly. I was thirsting, but not to go into battle. It started to mist about eleven o'clock; the sun shone through the cloud in a

red ball of fire, growing gradually dimmer and dimmer and throwing out weird fingers of light through the clouds. We could catch sight of the slanting lines of rain across the valleys before they hit us, which they soon did in violent showers. Columns of troops were coming back—New England boys of the 26th Division. We talked with some of them at the halts.

One big fellow told me, while he dipped water out of a puddle with a canvas bucket and filled a steaming Ford, that the 26th had made an attack that morning. The loss of life had been tremendous, as the Germans had defended every wood and thicket with their carefully placed machine guns. Not until the 75's had been brought up and used almost point-blank against the woods on the opposite ridge had "Fritz" given way. Then our men followed. There had been some bayonet work, of which more hereafter.

But "Fritz" had gone. Our brigade had come in just too late. We were to have reënforced the attack, and it was for this that we had made the killing march. How it was with the others I do not know, but personally I have always felt that I should never have had the courage that morning, when we were so weak with hunger, to make an attack. Courage is not a fixed quantity—only with a few—they are the born leaders. Only total physical collapse or death stops them.

The colonel and his staff turned aside at another big farm and there, with the headquarters company, went into billets. We literally tottered on a little farther under a soaking cold rain. Then on through a gate, across a muddy field, great shaggy masses of clay and grass attaching themselves to our shoes till we had to pry the clods off, the men taking their bayonets. Everything and everybody was streaming rain from every angle. It fell straight and cold, ran trickling down one's back under the pack, and finally soaked us until the clammy clothes stuck to the shivering skin. I looked back and saw our cookers following, a great consolation. What we needed was something to eat.

As usual, a patch of forest was to be our halting place for the night. The platoons filed into the rotten, muddy thicket. Nick began putting up my pup tent right away. The forest was too much cut up to attempt to camp the men in lines. Tents were scattered around on the higher spots everywhere, the men working doggedly and dully in the streaming rain. Above the sound of the water on the leaves, I could hear the clink and tapping of driving tent pegs. Pretty soon the trample of hoofs, sound of blows, swearing and cries announced the arrival of the kitchens and carts. Nick got my bedding roll, and over a can of alcohol heated some soup. I drank it steaming hot and crawled into my dry bed, not forgetting to hang my puttees and shoes near by. Never had I been so tired. Glen came and joined me. Lieutenant Scott and the captain were preparing to do the same. I was too done out to try to look after the men even, but I fell asleep worrying about them.

The hot soup suffused a luxurious warmth. Aches

and pains grew less, and through the trees the pungent smoke of green, wet wood began to drift from the kitchen. Thank God! the cooks were not too tired to cook. Meanwhile, the rain streamed on the dripping forest, the mud grew deeper, and the "army" slept.

Not even a gas sentinel was posted.

CHAPTER VII

GERMAN DUGOUTS

I AWOKE to hear the pleasant clinking of mess pans. The rain had stopped, but the forest was still dripping, and the mud was deep and peculiarly slippery. The captain and I crawled out, both about the same time, and made our way to the kitchen where a savory mess was being dished out, smoking hot gobs of bread and canned sweet potato, a favorite and frequent delicacy at the front. Paul and some of the other French soldiers were helping. By this time the men were happy again. A little rest and some-

thing to eat were doing wonders. The captain and
I were not much behind the rest of the company as
trenchermen, although I avoided eating much meat
at the front.

We were issued beef in immense quantities, sometimes having to bury a whole quarter of it. It became tainted very easily, where of course there was
no possible means of refrigeration. This meat ration
came wrapped in burlap, generally reasonably fresh;
but once open, it had to be carried around in the
ration carts, and unless quickly cooked, it spoiled very
rapidly, especially in those summer days along the
Marne when the sun was hot.

Another thing which hastened the destruction of
perishable food was the immense amount of decay
all along the front. All those rotten woods were filled
with dead horses, dead men, the refuse, excrement
and the garbage of armies. The ground must have
been literally alive with pus and decay germs.
Scratch your hand, cut yourself in shaving, or get
a little abrasion on your foot, and almost anything
could happen. Bichloride tablets were invaluable;
I always threw one into my canvas basin for good
luck.

During the meal, Lieutenant Scott, who had been
assistant division gas officer for a while, but who
had now returned to the company, joined us, and
mentioned that he was making all arrangements for
a new gas alarm, having found some empty brass

shells used for that purpose "over there"—and he pointed to a cape of trees that ran out from a wood-island into the surrounding fields.

That part of the world consisted of a great level plateau, prairie-like fields interspersed with woods, the "bois" of the French maps, like islands of all sizes and shapes. We were then camped in one of these wood "islands," and across "there," where the lieutenant had pointed, was another "island" in which were the remnants of a German battery. The captain and I strolled across after dinner, letting the warm sun dry us off.

The guns were still in their pits, as "Fritz" had left very suddenly here. The guns pointed their noses up at a high angle like hounds baying the moon, but they were silent now. The wood was full of little dugouts, walks, and houses. The Germans had evidently stayed here a long time. Out in the field were a large number of big shell craters in a line, *one, two, three* . . . where our 220's had evidently been ranging on the battery. They had come quite near, within fifty yards or so.

Along the edge of these thickets were a number of graves. I was greatly impressed by them. The crosses were well carved out of new wood, and the grave mounds carefully spaded. Here were wreaths of wax flowers, evidently sent from home, and a board giving the epitaph of the deceased, with his rank and honors: "He was a good Christian and fell in France fighting for the Fatherland, *Hier ruht in Gott.*" Verily, these seemed to be the same Goths and Vandals who left their graves even in Egypt; unchanged since the days of Rome, and still fighting her civilization, the woods-people against the Latins. Only the illuminating literary curiosity of a Tacitus was lacking to make the inward state of man visible by the delineation of the images of outer things.

We entered some of the dugouts, small, moundlike structures with straw inside. Some of the officers' were larger. There was a little beer garden in the middle of the wood with a chapel and a wreathed cross near by, white stones and twisting "rustic" paths. The railings and booths along these paths were made from roots and branches cleverly bent and woven, and sometimes carved. It reminded me of American "porch furniture" of a certain type. All quite German. Cast-off boots, shell-timers, one or two coats, and shrapnel-bitten helmets lay about with round Boche hats, "the little round button on top." Picture post-cards and magazines, pistol holsters, and one or two broken rifles completed this cartoon of invasion.

All the litter of material thus left behind was useless. I noticed the pictures of some fat, and rather jolly-looking German girls, and piles of a vast quantity of shells. We looked around thoroughly, but were very wary of traps. I remember making up my mind to make for one of these dugouts in case we were shelled. One always kept a weather eye open. About all this stuff there was at that time the dire taint of danger. Somehow everything German gave one the creeps. It was connected so intimately with all that was unpleasant, and associated so inevitably with organized fear, that one scarce regarded its owners as men. It seemed *then* as if we were fighting some strange, ruthless, insect-beings from another planet; that we had stumbled upon their nests after smoking them out. One had the same feeling as when waking up at night and realizing that there are rats under the bed.

The captain and I walked along the edge of the wood, encountering our French contingent on the way. They were "at home" in an old German dugout, happily squatted around several small fires, preparing their meal as *they* liked it. After a good deal of difficulty, they had prevailed on our mess sergeant to issue them their rations in bulk so that they could do their own cooking. Such little differences of customs are in reality most profound. Our physical habits were more like the Germans'!

The non-commissioned gas officer picked us up here. He was carrying back the big brass shell for a gas alarm. It gave forth a mellow musical note when touched with a bar of iron or a bayonet. The Germans had used this one themselves for that purpose, so it already had the holes and wire for suspending it.

Toward the Flame

The sergeant regaled us with the tale of a battalion of women machine gunners seen among the "Boche." They were said to have worked their guns to the last, of course, and to have died like true Amazons. I heard this story several times, but was never able to run it down. It was part of the romantic male gossip of the battle front. It grew very circumstantial as time went on. Occasionally pictures of German girls in uniforms would turn up in the dugouts, which may have been responsible for the origin of the tale. Besides, it was *such* a nice story. Every soldier would like to tame an Amazon. . . . We had been away from women now for several weeks. Members of the tribe of Amazons are to be encountered only upon "the confines of glamour and of sleep."

Nothing happened that night. We were even out of hearing of the guns, although a flickering could be seen in the sky in the direction of Rheims. Glen and I took some time off censoring letters, and trying to get the company clerk to put some forwarding addresses on the hospital mail, which had accumulated to the extent of several basketsful. It was now a nuisance to cart around. Some of this mail must have been destroyed on the sly by harassed company clerks. Our clerk *was* a clerk, in every sense of the word. War was not in his line, and ever since the severe shelling in "Death Valley," he had let his work slide. He was simply in a state of collapse. I would often find him weeping, and was truly very

sorry for the poor chap, but I could really do nothing
for him. He was not acquainted with Lord Tenny-
son's remarks on tears.

We moved before it was light, which is very early
in summer time in France. The dim columns of men
coming out of the woods, the lines of carts and kitchens assembling in the early, gray dawn, all without
a light, and generally pretty silently, was always
impressive.

In a few minutes we were headed back in the direction from which we had come. There was a full
moon, or one nearly so, hanging low in the west. As
I jolted along, on legs that seemed more like stilts
than limbs with knees, the heavy equipment sagged
at every step, and seemed to clink one's teeth together
weakly. At last the weariness and the jangle took
on a fagged rhythm that for me fell into the comfort
of rhyme.

We were beginning to be pretty tired by now and
even here needed relief. One no longer got up in
the morning full of energy. Hunger, dirt, and strain
were telling, and we felt more or less "all in" that day
in particular. One was consciously weak.

Nevertheless the country was beautiful; the full
moon just sinking in the west looked across the
smoking, misty valleys at the rising sun. There was
a gorgeous bloody-gold color in the sky, and the
woods and fields sparkled deliciously green, looking
at a little distance fresh and untouched. But that

was only a distant appearance, for this was the country over which two days before the Americans had driven the Germans from one machine gun nest to another, and on from crest to crest. A nearer approach showed the snapped tree-trunks, the tossed branches and shell-pitted ground, and at one halt that we made, Nick called me down a little slope to see something.

There was a small spring in a draw beside the road, where two Germans were lying. One was a big, brawny fellow with a brown beard, and the other a mere lad. He looked to be about 14 or 15 with a pathetically childish chin, but he carried potato-masher bombs. They had evidently stopped here to try to fill their canteens, probably both desperate with thirst, when they were overtaken by our men. The young boy must have sheltered himself behind the man while the latter held our fellows back a little. There was a scorched place up the side of the ravine where a hand grenade had exploded, but the big German had been surrounded, and killed by the bayonet right through his chest. His hands were still clutching at the place where the steel had gone through. He was one of the few I ever saw who had been killed by the bayonet. The boy was lying just behind him. His back appeared to have been broken, probably by a blow with the butt of a rifle, and he was contorted into a kind of arch, only his feet and shoulders resting on the ground. It was he who had probably thrown the grenade that had exploded near by. The little spring had evidently been visited by the wounded, as there were blood and first-aid wrappings about. I refused to have the company water tank filled there.

Our water was carried in a two-horse cart with a seat for the driver and a large barrel-like tank of steel behind. This had a hand pump for sucking the liquid into the tank, and brass spigots at the rear to draw it off. Getting a good water supply was always a problem and often impossible. It was best to drink only the boiled water of the coffee ration.

We passed a great field that morning that was rapidly filling up with artillery. There was evidently a concentration on of some kind. Battery after battery could be seen moving up a side road for miles, and the guns were being placed about in all the fields and woods. In most cases no effort was made to camouflage them. Once in a while from under some tree, or from the edge of a wood, would come that characteristic white puff and blinding flash, to be followed a distinct moment later by a blow of sound. The horses, the lines of caissons, and all the paraphernalia of artillery marshaled in the fields made a great impression. To the poor "doughboy," there is always something luxurious about artillery.

Toward noon we came into a little village—just a few ruined houses scattered along the road, still full of German relics and signs. A few men began to pick about among the ruins like chickens who don't expect to find anything. There was an old spring bed in one house, which some one carried out. About twelve men tried to sit on it all at one time.

Here we again ran across some of the 26th U. S. Division. At that time they had seen so much more fighting than we, that they seemed veterans, by comparison. Their clothes were in very bad shape, the set expression of their faces, and their small platoons advertised what they had been through. They sat along the roads and told us stories of the fights and recounted details of their losses. I thought it disheartening for our men, but the "Yanks" did not seem to feel that way about it. They held an abso-

lutely fatalistic viewpoint, telling us we would never get through the game. "Wait," they said, "wait." Later on I understood. There was a great pride about these fellows.

Men who have faced death often and habitually can never again have the same attitude towards life. It is hard to be enthusiastic about little things again. The fact that everybody is soon going to die is a little more patent than before. One sees behind the scenes, the flowers and the grave-blinds, the opiate of words read from the Good Book, and the prayers. For there is Death, quiet, calm, invincible, and there is no escape. Yet there are compensations.

For instance, one loses one's horror of the dead themselves. They have so patently lost all personality, and to the soldier, the process of their incorporation with the mineral kingdom is a visible one. Earth is claiming them again. It is my honest opinion, a very humble one, that the sight of battlefields must always be a great blow to the lingering belief in personal immortality. The least that can be said is that the subject was never mentioned by any one, contrary to the statements of religious enthusiasts and the stock cant of journalism.

There is no man who is so totally absorbed by the present as the soldier. It claims all his attention and he lives from moment to moment in times of danger with an animal keenness that absorbs him utterly. This is a happy and saving thing. With time to brood, conditions would often seem intolerable. To the soldier, *now* is everything. It is in the piping times of peace and leisure that man has had the time to afford himself the luxury of an immortal soul. When the present world is not engrossing enough, we begin to ponder on another.

After lying around in the little town for an hour or so, some of the 26th began to troop back. They had been taken out to make an attack, but found that

"Fritz" had not waited and they were naturally in high spirits. One red-headed chap had found a big German breastplate, and was wearing that and a huge, painted helmet that he doffed now and then to the vast joy of everybody he passed. He looked like Sancho Panza, and roars of laughter and chaff followed him up the road: "Where did you get that hat?" and "Look out you don't fall overboard with that iron life-preserver," or, "Where's the stove lid for the seat of your pants?" etc., etc. To the American there is something humorous about armor; to him it is always a stage property, not to be confused with a real protective article of apparel such as an undershirt. Even the "tin hat" was taken doubtfully at first. Only experience justified it.

For some reason orders were changed here. Instead of going on, after we got the order to fall in we countermarched, and then turned aside into the usual field to bivouac in the inevitable wood. Some of the 26th were also sharing with us these woods which were usually dirty. Apparently a great number of "outfits" had camped here from time to time; some for a considerable period I judged. The holes which the men had dug for themselves were full of old straw and newspapers. I found a Chicago *Tribune* which was the first newspaper I had seen for some time. It was six weeks old or more. I read even the advertisements with great pleasure. They seemed to breathe a reality and matter-of-factness about "home" that was delightful just then.

The kitchens drew up right beside the woods here, and cooked lunch quickly, while the captain and I rested on some old hospital litters that had been abandoned in the woods. Some one had stolen a good bed for a night or two.

That wood was one of the most "war-like" places I ever saw. The litter of trash, newspapers, clothes, old rifles, shoes, and all kinds of articles, together with the pockmarked effect of the straw-filled holes through the broken tangle of saplings and weeds, gave an indescribably clatty atmosphere to the place. Out in the field, here and there, the men were relieving themselves or squatting down, stripped to the waist, carefuly picking the vermin out of their undershirts. There were a few dead horses about and I suspected the water we drank. The "romance and glamour of war" were certainly lacking here.

During lunch the captain told me that an advance, probably with an attack, was on for that afternoon. Somehow the idea rather spoiled the meal. The other two battalions had already gone ahead it seemed. We had lost touch with them, and were to move forward in support. The major had intrusted "B" company with acting as advance, and I was instructed to take charge of the "point." A few minutes later we started.

Toward the Flame

The major at the last moment changed all the orders which the captain had given me, and handed me a map as we moved out which had nothing whatever marked on it. He told me our objective, a town called Courpoil, and said we were to proceed by way of Epieds where the enemy had been in great force that morning.

From his manner and description I thought that we were moving through hostile country and so sent my flankers out on either side into the fields, with the "point," a corporal and a man, a considerable distance ahead. I kept some men near me to keep in touch with the rear if necessary.

At the risk of being a bit tedious, I am going to relate the details of this march to show that in a great many cases so-called military "science" and training simply give a man a preconceived idea of how a thing should be done, until in his eyes the method is more important than the result. Both the captain and the major were too well read in minor tactics, and had attended too many schools to be able to conduct even the simplest of operations without the most elaborate procedure. To the very last, they played at war like the men in the textbooks. Both of them meant well, but others died.

The captain had an "ideal" advance guard in his head. According to him, it must be disposed like a triangle; while the major, God bless him! was strong for flankers. Finally the major called me back. He

and the captain had evidently been having an argument over it and were both very angry. The major wanted to know why I hadn't gone with the point, the most advanced party. He said he always expected his lieutenants to be "leaders," or words to that effect. Now neither the captain nor major could speak a word of French, and in the meantime I had talked with a number of returning French wagoners who gave me some real information. I knew that the enemy had abandoned Epieds and were miles ahead. Leaving them with this new thought to digest, I returned to the point which I now heroically led according to the major's order, knowing the enemy to be at least ten miles away.

Men have been decorated for less—if I had only been a chaplain!

We turned down the road at right angles, following the map, but at the corner our scout officer came up and excitedly begged me not to do this, as he had some other theory about our route. It was just nearly right enough to be confusing, and I had to argue with him in order to convince myself I was right. Just then arrived one runner each from the captain and the major with contrary orders about disposing the advance party. I returned a sedative answer to both officers and determined to take things in my own hands and *move ahead,* or we would never get anywhere. So I turned the corner and went on.

It was a beautiful, sunny afternoon and we were moving over a rolling country dotted here and there with wood-islets and, in the distance, a range of hills. There was a long white ribbon of road with green fields on either side that led down a gradual hill with a little town at the bottom of the slope.

A few minutes later we entered this and found it jammed with French wagon trains, not *camions,* but horse-drawn wagons. The place had been slightly shelled, and there was still a big German sign across the road, *"Nach Herrenhausen,"* which was the synthetic name they had given to some little French village. The congestion in the one little street, which, by the way, twisted at right angles twice,

126

was terrific. Some of the French had halted and were watering their horses at a small cross-marked fountain; others had unhitched, and had their horses tied along the street with the wagons standing there. Men were sleeping everywhere, on the doorsteps, under the wagons; and one could look in the half-destroyed houses and see the *poilus* cooking. Some of the old German camouflage rags were still waving over the streets. It looked as though long, long ago there had been a gala day here, but now—the circus was over. The big show had, indeed, moved on.

At the corners I posted men to warn our fellows which way to turn as they came along, but just in the middle of the town we met another wagon train on its way back, driving at a fast clip. The French can drive, but expect you to get out of their way. I saw trouble ahead when they met the main body of the battalion; some one would have to stop. There would be a mess.

Sure enough, about halfway up the hill an order came to halt, as the battalion was unable to get through the town. I had sent a message back to them warning them of the congestion in the town, but it had never occurred to our "well-trained" officers to go around it.

About half an hour later the captain came up. He was very angry about something and made a pass at one of the men. The rest laughed. I suppose a continuation of the advance-guard argument had caused this. The major must have prevailed as there were *lots* of flankers. A platoon went out on either side to scout the roads—full of nothing but French wagon trains. When we started to advance again I had to stop every few minutes to let our flankers catch up because in the fields they had harder going than on the road. This, of course, delayed the whole brigade. Finally, to my great relief, a motorcycle runner came up with a direct order from General Weigel, whose car had just appeared in the rear, to push on without delay.

By this time, we were descending the hill towards Epieds which lay on a crossroads at the bottom of a little valley.

The day before there had been a desperate fight in and about Epieds. The little town was the worst-shelled village that we had seen up to this time. Our own artillery, and afterwards the guns of the re-treating invader, had literally knocked the place to pieces. Whole lines of houses were down, and one could tell by the débris, shells, wrecked machine guns, and machine gun belts scattered here and there what an obstinate hand-to-hand combat it had been. Places were still smoking in the ruins where hand grenades had been used. In one little garden I glanced at, there were still a lot of dead men, and the snout of a machine gun was sticking through a wall. The church at the corner had immense shell-holes in it, and I think there was a headquarters or dressing station here, as there was a good deal of coming and going. Across the street a house was burning, and some French soldiers were trying to put it out in a languid sort of way.

The road turned again at Epieds and we started going up a long hill. On one side of the dale was a huge, empty-windowed château staring across the valley-lands and frightfully shot up and ruined.

Our artillery fire had evidently overtaken the retreating enemy about here. There were dead horses and human remains along the road, and hundreds of shell-holes. The camouflage screen of old, brown trees, which had stretched along the road for a mile, was blasted away, and in one place a German had been blown clear off the road and hung on the sagging wire. Shrapnel had come along afterwards and literally shredded him. He had no head but, strangely enough, held his helmet in his hands. He was blood-soaked and his bowels were hanging out. The horses lay about in all sorts of contortions. I was sorry for them. A number of the queer barge-like German wagons had been abandoned here. Under the seat of one was a well-thumbed Bible which one of my sergeants took.

I looked back and saw that the general's car was coming up near the head of the column. Putting the glass on it, I could even see him and his staff. This was one of the few occasions where I really found a use for the double "E" binocular. Moving over the hills with the "point," they were excellent to search out just what was going on. The occupation of little groups of men and the stir around small towns or camps stood out startlingly clear as the glass was put on them.

Somehow an exaltation came to us that afternoon after we got up out of the death-strewn valley and found ourselves walking over the clear, wind-swept hills. The men felt it, too. We had a few songs, and pressed on fast and merrily, always anxious to see what was over the next crest. At last we came up onto a plateau with little woods in the foreground and in the distance one long, unbroken line of forest. It was the Bois de la Fère. In that, somewhere, were the other two battalions of the regiment.

One of the men pointed out a balloon to me, and as we gathered around to look at it through the glass, there came a nasty rattle of machine guns and the faint bump of shells bursting away off. In one place there was a white smoke going up from among the trees. I sent a runner back to warn the commanding officer about the balloon, which I felt pretty sure must be in the German lines. Farther along the road we could also make out the red tiles on the roofs of a town nestled amid the trees. I passed on, and was rather surprised to see the general's gray car coming right up the hill after us.

It was already far ahead of the leading battalion.

CHAPTER VIII

COURPOIL

THE little town just ahead of us was a place called Courpoil, already occupied by the French.

It should be borne in mind that from the Marne to the Vesle the Americans were incorporated with the French Army; that is, the French generals had charge of the major operations, the details, of course, being left to our own officers. It is only just to add, in view of recent criticism, that all during this time our respect, liking and admiration for the French were unqualified. The good nature of the *poilu* is apparently inexhaustible, and the French officer is nearly always a gentleman, in all ordinary contacts at least, which is not so universally true in our army, unfortunately.

One of the French officers informed me, as we entered Courpoil, that we were under direct observation, adding that the balloon I had seen farther back was a German "sausage." He looked rather anxiously at the general's automobile snorting up the hill. We moved on farther till the road took a turn. Some of the French were lying along it, but they got up and ran among the houses as we approached. There was the far-off roar and groaning shriek of a shell and a deafening explosion about one hundred yards down the road. The enemy had certainly seen us. Shell after shell continued to arrive. Why they did not toss them into the town I did not understand.

I sent back the signal to halt, as it was manifestly impossible to proceed down that particular road, and then took shelter with the rest of the "point" behind the most solid stone house I could find, where I could wait for orders. There I could look about me.

Courpoil was just an ordinary French village, its houses built closely up to and along the road. They were now torn by shell fire. A good many of them, however, were still in fair shape. I could see some of the French soldiers upstairs. Smoke was coming out of one of the chimneys, and looking out across the fields along a sort of low ridge, I saw the reserve

line of the French stretching away, their blue helmets bobbing about like so many turtles among the
shell-holes. Now and then a group would get up and
move forward across the fields towards a line of little
copses, or wood-islets, a few hundred yards ahead.
An "infiltration" was in progress.

We were far out of rifle shot here, but in fine artillery range. "Fritz" was shelling with his 6 and 3
inch, and somewhere back in the Bois de la Fère,
whose sea of trees we could overlook from Courpoil,
there was the short vicious bark of an Austrian 77
every few minutes. Once in a while, there would be
a brief burst of rifle and machine gun firing. Otherwise, it was a rather warm, pleasant July day with
the wind in the trees.

Just then
t h e gen-
eral's c a r
came over
the brow
of the hill
and t o r e
i n t o the
town, fol-
lowed by
our whole
battalion.
A French
officer ran

133

up to remonstrate about the automobile, but I told him it was *un général américain.*

"Mon Dieu," said he, *"au revoir."*

The General stuck his head out of the window and asked me about the situation. I told him all I knew: *"Boches est là,"* was all the French had told me, pointing east.

"Jump in," said the general.

I hated to do it.

We cut right out into the fields along a sort of cow lane in full view of the balloon, and finally stopped behind a little clump of trees. There were a few French in a shell-hole near by who got right up and moved out. By the time the battalion had arrived and was halted in the town, "Fritz" knew that "something" was going on. They must, of course, have seen the automobile. A few shells skipped up the road where the machine had been. I could see our men scatter.

The general and all of us swarmed out and made along the ridge for about a quarter of a mile, leaving the car in the trees. There in a wide field we came across a shelter, logs piled across a ditch with rocks on top. The inside was a shell-hole. There was another brigadier-general in it with a telephone and an adjutant. He was a general of artillery, part of whose brigade was posted in the woods behind us, and the rest, "coming up," as he expressed it, a whole regiment of 120's on the way. Whether our general expected to meet him there or not I don't know. The Artillery told us "the situation":

The two other battalions of our regiment with the colonel and some of the French were "lost", and apparently cut off in the Bois de la Fère, which our artillery was of course afraid to shell. They, the battalions, were supposed to be near a place called Croix Rouge Farm about five or six miles away, but nothing definite had been heard of them since early that morning. Of the exact location of French, Germans, or Americans, no one knew anything for certain. Our own men had not moved up yet.

General Weigel sent me back to tell the major to bring the battalion up, which was done. The men were scattered out by companies and platoons through the fields like the French. Some of them started to dig in. A little later the kitchens and carts came up through the town at a spanking clip and bumped out over the fields into some woods about a quarter of a mile in the rear. Our men kept moving up and down the crest, and the shelling became pretty lively. The French moved forward. In the town a shell fell every few seconds with a monotonous whistle and regularity. Despite this, a dressing station was established there in a house.

After a little struggle with myself I determined to go and try to locate the two battalions. The plan of the general was to bring them back and form a general line with our battalion. I volunteered to carry the orders. He gave me a map with very little or no data on it, and I started out, heading along the ridge for some distance, in order to avoid the shelled areas near the town. It was then about four o'clock in the afternoon.

Directly in front and eastward lay a broad wheat-field on the other side of which were little spaces of dense woods. Far away over these peered the ugly nose of the German balloon. Off to the right loomed the dense forest of La Fère, and behind was the country of little fields, rolling hills, and thickets through which we had just come.

I had hardly gone half a mile when out of one of these thickets appeared about twenty of our own men, led by Lieutenant Fletcher. Fletcher had been a teacher of philosophy at home and despite the fact was also somewhat of a philosopher himself, so I was quite shocked at his appearance. He was obviously used up; nearly numb with fatigue and anxiety, he said.

Fletcher was scout officer of one of our lost battalions. He and his scouts had been looking for it since early morning without success. They had found some wounded men and some stragglers who had told them that the two battalions had run into a lot of machine gun nests and heavy artillery fire in the forest and were suffering heavy losses. That the colonel was right on the firing line with the men, that there was nothing to eat, and that ammunition was running low, was also part of their story as well as it could be pieced together.

Discounting these tales as much as I dared, the situation still looked bad. Also I began to feel a little worried about myself, an unimportant but obtrusive consideration. I questioned some of the tired men further, and managed to get some idea of direction and distance out of their combined evidence.

" 'F' company is down there," said one lad, pointing to a patch of woods about a mile away.

A sudden burst of shelling in that direction confirmed me in thinking that something *was* down "that-a-way," so I started. Fletcher started with me, but was so tired that he stumbled several times. Finally I drew up and argued with him, pointing out that his real duty was to take his men back to General Weigel and report to him, as they were all in, and the general would want what information he had at that time. The scout detail of the second battalion, which had also been searching the woods, joined us here with the same story. I told them it would obviously be the general's desire that they should report to him; informed them where he was, and went on. Fletcher went back to his men rather unwillingly. I never saw any one so tired. He must have covered an immense distance trying to make *liaison* that day.

I cut directly across the wheat field towards the woods where "F" company was supposed to be. The grain was ripe. There was a great space of it there rippling under the afternoon sun, but it made hard going. The whole area was being gently shelled, but the chance of a man's being hit in a field like that was too remote to be considered. Nevertheless, one considered it.

Just as I got down to the edge of the woods there were several shells dropped into it. I could hear the trees crashing, and was greatly surprised to see a crowd of our men run out and then stop in the field and look around. Some sat down. Soon the field was all dotted with little groups. Then some more shells fell, and some more men came out. This happened two or three times. On questioning the men I found they were a company of our own regiment. No one seemed to be in charge. It was just like a picnic sitting around in a field.

I want to digress here, just in case some very "tactical" person should ever read this book, to tell them that this same company was one of the most faithful that ever served the United States. Later on the captain was killed leading his men. All of this particular day they had been cleaning out machine guns in the Bois de la Fère. Fighting here was a great man hunt, every little group for itself. In the dense coverts all control was impossible. Here is where the startling quality of our men came out. Whenever "two or three of them were gathered together," the fight went grimly on. Even the lonely individual stuck to it, and somehow sooner or later, we went forward.

It was the grim common sense of the "doughboy" and not our obsolete and impossible tactics that won us ground. Oh! the precious time wasted in our elaborate, useless, murderous "science" called "musketry." It is as much out of style as the musket from which it takes its name. Teaching it should be made a court-martial offense. It is murder in print. Battles were not fought in lines.

We forgot the trenches, too, and simply moved forward in groups right through the cow lots, the little villages and the woods, meeting "Fritz" in cellars, in old outhouses, along road ditches, ensconced in the middle of yon fine looking tree, hid in a hole

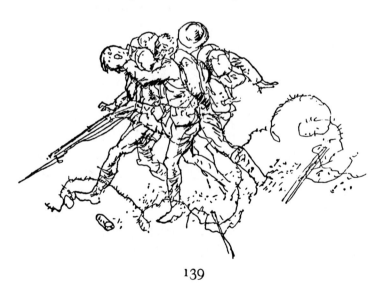

behind a coal heap, or in a haystack, waiting till we had passed, and shooting us in the back. Sometimes he lurked in a patch of weeds or in a pleasant green woods, but never in line, seldom in force in any one place, always doing the unexpected thing, and doing it bravely and well.

Let us give even the Devil his due, such a wonderful, delaying, rear-guard action was never seen, save Mons! With machine gunners and his marvelous artillery, "Fritz" held the world back for months and died game, magazine stories written from rearward dugouts and Paris to the contrary notwithstanding. I disliked the Germans, but I disliked them because I feared them, knowing full well their deadly capability. They had crushed individualism so thoroughly that they had the bravery and determination of insects. That is why their courage was not entirely admirable. But to resume:

By and by the captain of the scattered company also came out of the woods and sat down in the field. Every one sat there doing nothing because there was nothing to do. They were dead, fagged out. The shells continued to smash among the trees. I went up to the captain and told him where our battalion and the general was. He could see our men moving along the little ridge, was much relieved to get his orders to join the general, and began filtering his men back. There was considerable difficulty in getting them off the ground where they were sitting.

Courpoil

Everybody was too tired apparently to care. Just what was the matter I do not know, as I had to move on. From some of the sergeants I got news of the other battalions. One of them sketched in for me on the map a road that I could follow.

I walked along the edge of the woods till it ran out in kind of a point into the field. There I met a medical corps chap coming across the wheat. He was carrying a message to "some one" for aid. I told him where our general was, and after pumping him dry of all information, learned that part of our lost men were only a mile or so away in the woods, but scattered through it in platoons and squads, and that heavy fighting was going on about Croix Rouge Farm. He also described to me the route he had followed. There were still Germans where he had crawled through, he said. I wrote a message telling General Weigel of what I had learned so far and informed him that I was pushing on. I sent it back by the medical man. We had this talk in a big shell-hole with a little shrapnel coming over now and then.

Greatly helped by this last information, I was now able to go ahead with more confidence. After crossing about a half mile of field on a kind of road marked by artillery wheels, I came into the outskirts of the Bois de la Fère. The edge of the wood had a dyke around it and a tangle of barbed wire. Getting through it was not so easy. After working through,

Toward the Flame

I saw an open path I might have followed and marked it with a newspaper. It was a Berlin paper of recent date.

Although it was past five o'clock, the late French sun was still shining brightly, long columns of light streaming down through the trees. It was very silent in the woods, and instinct made me move quietly as soon as I entered them.

Just at this point there was a small village of dugouts, little mounds of logs and stones covered with earth. A German machine gun outfit had been here, judging by the abandoned material. Souvenir hunters would have smacked their lips. I was much interested myself, and entered two or three. Somehow they impressed me as having been abandoned only a few minutes. I grew more cautious; the feeling of the nearness of danger overcame me. I was afraid to step out of the dugout I had entered last, and drew my pistol in a kind of panic. There were two rooms in this one with a kind of door between. When I went into the other room I got a distinct shock and felt sure there must be some one there. There was stale tobacco smoke still in the air! This was one of the most profound scares I ever got. In the middle of the quiet woods in that lonely room, full of smoke that some German had just blown out of his face a few minutes before, I stood still a long time, listening for footsteps and to my own heartbeat. But no one came. I got out of there like a child out of a dark room and went on, sneaking very carefully down the path.

Pretty soon I came on a lake glistening through the trees. On the far side there were a couple of good-looking brick farmhouses with some of our men moving about them. A stretcher was carried up, and I saw a doctor with his white armband come to the door. Just then I saw my Germans, too.

They were about two hundred yards ahead of me down the path, and moving off very stealthily through the trees. They were carrying a tripod, not a machine gun, and their helmets, I could see, were painted with yellow and green spots like the sunlight through the leaves. One broke away from the others and started to run. After a while they all faded into the shadows of the woods, but I took great care, moving from tree to tree, afraid of snipers.

It took me about half an hour thus to work down to the farmhouses. I had found a dressing station, as I surmised, with our fellows moving around freely among the houses. It had been a German command post a few hours before. There was a splendid deep dugout in the rear. Our men were getting souvenirs. About half a platoon of "L" company was sitting along the edge of the wood near the lake kicking their heels. I learned from them that the rest of the company was up one of the many little roads through the forest that branched away at this point, and that they were coming our way.

Sure enough, a few minutes later the other platoons emerged from the trees, led by their captain. They had been pretty roughly handled in the forest, losing some men by shells, and running into some bad machine gun trouble. Captain Keel was very glad to hear where our battalion was, and led his men out of the woods and up to the new line as the general desired. My friend Wyke, who had been in the forest with them, described later on some of their experiences:

"I was doing some scouting on my own account when I heard a noise and, looking up one of the roads through the woods, saw a party of horsemen coming down it. As I knew that we had no cavalry, I ducked, and ducked quick! It was a party of Germans, about twelve of them, mounted, and carrying two or three machine guns. They passed me talking low, but laughing and joking. Evidently they thought it good fun to shoot up our fellows, and then leave them to laboriously crawl around trying to locate the machine gun nest. They were going to the rear. I kept low in the ditch by the side of the road, and they rode by me and never saw me, although I could almost have touched them. Just about this time some of 'L' company came wandering up the road in single file. They had not gone very far when a shell burst right in front of them. Some of them squatted right where they were, but one chap ran back along the road. As usual the enemy acted

on the theory that somebody would be running to
the rear and skipped shells up the road. It seemed
as if they were chasing this man, who yelled. Then
we heard another shell coming. He heard it too and
ran screaming. Then he ducked, but too late. It
got him. There wasn't any use burying him. I went
up to the rest of the men and got them together and
pushed forward. The shells went through the woods
back of us. There was only a corporal with the
squad. A little later I saw Captain Keel and 'kidded'
him about the way his men went after things. He
didn't like it."

This is my friend's conversation verbatim.* I give

* From a notebook memorandum made at the time.

it to show a little glimpse of what went on in those woods. "Now what should Sergeant Doe have done?" as the tactic books say. Well, what should he?

By now, however, two companies, "L" and "F," were both out of the woods, so I felt somewhat encouraged. A bewildering thing at this forest farm was to find men from nearly all the other companies. They each had a different version of the state of affairs, so there was only one thing to do. Go and see for myself.

To tell the whole story of that evening and night would be monotonous, but it was a very exciting one for me. When dark came on I had to be doubly cautious. There were groups of men all through the woods, mostly our own, but they were along the paths for the most part. I avoided all of them, as I was afraid of being mistaken for a German. I could tell by the muttered conversation. Once, and once only, I heard German, but French several times. Mostly it was deadly quiet. You might expect to find groups in pockets and ravines. I could hear the firing at Croix Rouge Farm, and this gave me my direction, as did also the moon. I had no compass, and would not have used it if I had. I simply worked toward the farm.

About eleven o'clock I came across a French major. He was eating bread and onions, but I was glad to see him, nevertheless. I had intended to work clear

146

up to Croix Rouge Farm, but to tell the truth my
nerves had given out and I was really afraid to go
farther without knowing where I was. The woods
with their shadows and sounds were too much for
me. Also I was weak from hunger and the miles
covered, and ate some of the major's bread and drank
of his wine with delight. Two or three other French
officers came around. In the middle of that forest
of death-traps, all awash with moon shadows, they
had not forgotten to be polite. I know they felt the
strain, because they were peculiarly alert, but they
shook hands, bade me welcome, and shared their food
and wine which must have been precious. I thanked
God my mother had made me learn a little French.
It saved some good French and American lives that
night. From the French I obtained information
which made further blundering through the forest
unnecessary.

The French major took my map and drew on it
the entire situation about Croix Rouge Farm. He
also showed me the German line as it had been at
six o'clock that evening, pointed out a town in front
of us, and told me the French were about to attack
it. I gave him what information of our positions
I had.

When I left him, I had a fairly clear story of the
whole forest laid out on my map. He was too clear
and certain about his information to leave any doubts
in my head about its not being correct; also it checked

up with mine. It took me only a short time to get back. I went straight to the rear, guided by a French soldier, till I got out of the woods and into the fields, picked out a farm road, and within an hour's time was at the general's headquarters in the shell-hole. The major wanted to see the map first, but I took it to the general. Time was important.

Both General Weigel and the general of artillery were eager to get the information. They said nothing to me, but asked a number of questions. They were soon drawing in the coördinates on the map for a barrage, and I heard enough to know that my work made it possible for them to do so. Otherwise we would have been held up much longer and the barrage might have fallen on our own men, for barrage there had to be. A good deal of shelling was still going on about Courpoil. Our men were all dug in in the wheat fields. One lad in "B" company had been wounded in the foot.

I went out and hunted up Nick. He was just finishing his hole, but he made it larger for me. I crawled into it with him. The warmth of his body was welcome, as I was cold and tired. I was just about to go to sleep when the captain came and told me I had been detailed to guide Major Smathers of the 109th Machine Gun Battalion down to the farm at the head of the lake. This took another hour and nearly did me out. The newspaper I had put at the path through the wire showed up white and saved us a lot of trouble. When I got back, I crawled in with Nick. Through the mist, the machine gunners with their little mule carts were just moving out in a long caravan-like line.

In a damp hole like this, one's warm, water-proof trench coat came in excellently, except that it left the feet uncovered. Again and again I had cause to bless it; but sleep was not to be that night. After about an hour's snooze in this damp grave, the captain again wakened me.

An attack was being planned. I was so sleepy, it hardly mattered. I went over to the major's hole and heard enough to learn that they didn't know the French were in front of us, or anything else about "the situation." The captain of "A" company, whose humor was devastating, began to joke them about it, and the captain of the headquarters company, which had just moved in to Courpoil, joined in. The major stood on his dignity, which was in this case purely official. All this was around one little shaded candle, with the shells going overhead. A great many technical terms were used, but no conclusions were reached, although maps were much in evidence. There seemed to be considerable difficulty in always getting them right side up. Wrangling ensued. Pennsylvania-ese mated with military French, begetting a strange mule-like jargon. Here was a quarrel about how to fight somebody else conducted in solecisms in which the premises of all parties to the controversy were entirely wrong. It was almost legally magnificent. It was more than that—it was military. I lit a cigarette.

Yet all this time I was too tired and sleepy to get up much interest even in an attack, although I went back and awakened the company and got them all in platoon order ready to move off. Nothing happened. The argument of the professional strategists was still going on, so I took the men and sheltered them in a ditch along the little cow road, keeping them together. They went to sleep by platoons. The candle was still burning in the major's dugout, but it was nearly down to the socket now. I looked out across the moonlit fields and through the night mist saw our machine gun battalion coming back like a file of ghosts. Evidently their major had discovered the uselessness of placing machine guns in a farmhouse in the middle of the woods with the French in front of him. I laughed heartily to myself. There would be no attack that night.

Nick and I turned in. The top sergeant joined us in our corner of the ditch and we slept the sleep of the just. When we woke it was a beautiful warm morning.

CHAPTER IX

AN AIR BATTLE

WE lay at Courpoil nearly a whole day. Since it was rather a typical day near the front, I shall narrate it in some detail.

In the morning I went over with the first sergeant and got a wash at the village fountain and talked to one of our surgeons who had a dressing station in a little house there. A lot of the wounded had been brought to him out of the woods during the night, and ambulances were tearing up and down the road. A shell had burst in front of the house early that

morning and torn a man's legs off. They generally
picked some place like this for a dressing station, a
crossroads or a church, or something equally conspicuous. This was easily found by our men, but also
easily located by the enemy. In many cases surgeons
who picked out such locations should have been rep-
rimanded for choosing them instead of decorated for
staying in them. A great many of our doctors and
others, be it said, were stupidly plucky; sometimes
exposed situations could not be avoided, however.

A great deal of ammunition and rations had now
been brought up to Courpoil, owing to the exertions
of our lieutenant colonel and the general, who had
already started some details through the forest to
relieve the hungry men there.

After a good wash in my canvas bucket, and a talk
with the doctor, I made off in the direction of the
kitchens ensconced in the shelter of a little wood
several hundred yards to the rear. The men were
just forming a mess line, clinking their pans as usual,
when there was a general scatterment as several airplanes dashed over the top of the trees. They proved
to be our own, however, and pretty soon down the
line one of our sausage balloons poked its nose up
out of the *bois.*

The mess sergeant had a surprise for us that morning. A real breakfast, good steak, and hot cakes with
syrup. I was so hungry that the cakes made an un-
dying impression on me. It is good to eat with an

appetite like that. Some of the pleasantest memories of the army are of sitting around on the ground talking and eating, while passing the time of day with a well-filled mess pan. It was a very pleasant green woods that morning with horses standing about cozily switching flies, and there were cigarettes, which tasted fine after breakfast. The men were in high spirits, too.

After breakfast, I went over and talked to Captain Haller and Lieutenant Kellar of "D" company. They were leaning back in a kind of leaf shelter made of logs, shelter-halves and branches. We gave each other the latest "wrong" rumors and then had the usual battalion gossiping bee. As we disliked the same persons, we had quite a basis of friendship to start with.

When I got back to the little ridge where the company had dug in, the major general and his staff had arrived to talk things over with our brigadier and the general of artillery. There were a number of staff officers about in "Sam Browne" belts which always looked curious at the front. The major general was wearing one and did not have a helmet. Our major's dugout and the general's were only a few feet apart in the field. The dugouts consisting, as stated, of a roofed-over hole in a drain. We could look over from "our ditch" behind the road and see the powwow of the bigwigs going on. It continued some time. You must imagine the men scattered along a general line in all kinds of holes, or sheltered in a rough series of trenches about waist deep, dug in the fields over-night.

About ten o'clock a whole regiment of artillery moved in. It was always a spectacle to watch the guns go by. These were very big howitzers, but horse-drawn. The men rode the lead horses, walked, or sat on the caissons. There was a rolling cloud of dust up to the horses' knees; some of them were re-markably fine gray beasts. The artillery cut across fields and took up position in the woods. Some 75's had just moved in. A battery of that caliber was just behind us. It looked to me as though the pieces were leveled right at us.

None of us gave much thought to these guns until an hour or two later, when there was a frightful roar that absolutely overpowered everything. This was followed by several minutes of intense "drum fire." Our barrage was on. The 75's just behind us were especially insistent and painfully near. Every time they fired, the wheat in front of them bowed down as though a sudden wind had passed over it. Soon there was the peculiar, acrid, thirsty taste of powder in the air.

As time went on it became possible to recognize the voices of the several guns. I noticed again the bell-tolling effect of the 75's, and the belching of the howitzers. A lot of metal was coming from away in the rear, too. We could hear the shells shrieking and wailing overhead, and there was a constant vibrant roar. All the leaves on the trees and the bushes were trembling. One had to shout to be heard. Suddenly all this ceased as instantly as it had begun.

A few minutes later there was a drone and a bang, and one poor little German shell broke in the field out in front. Every one laughed, partly from relief at our own noise being over. The 75's behind us immediately started in and fired away again. Then two or three more German shells came skipping over the fields right in line toward the officers' dugout. There was a general scatterment. Again the 75's.

The U. S. 42nd, the famous "Rainbow Division," came up to relieve us that day. They had come from the Toul Sector, where they had been in trenches, and this open warfare was at first new to them. Some of their units passed us, marching along the little road where we lay along the ridge. We noted the six months' foreign service stripes on their sleeves, at that time un-

usual in our army, as well as the fact that they were carrying unusually large and heavy packs with a lot of cooking utensils. There was a lavish profusion of pots and pans. The trench life they had been leading must have been very different from our backwoods, gypsy existence of constant moves. At that time the "Rainbow" did not look nearly as war-worn as the 26th, at least that was our impression.

After lunch we had the most exciting incident of a rather interesting day. Our observation balloon, which was hanging over the trees about a mile away, was evidently troubling the Germans, because about three o'clock two enemy planes came over to put an end to it. They were met by three or four of ours and we could hear the machine guns talking madly.

Everybody took a crack at "Fritz" as he came past. It sounded like an immense number of firecrackers going off, rifles, even pistols; and under it all droned the steady rivet-hammer *rip-rip-rip-rip* of the machine guns.

The planes circled around over the woods like a flock of fighting birds, and then suddenly one black plane broke away and made a swoop towards the balloon, which was being frantically pulled down. The German dived straight for it, shooting into it. Immediately we saw the little black figure of the observer dive out, followed by a long, streaming, white thing that suddenly broke into a mushroom shape. The parachute with the man clinging to it was blown quite a distance and drifted down among the trees, while the balloon began to give forth a tremendous volume of white smoke. Then it burst into an immense white flame, with flaming strips falling toward the ground, trailing wisps of smoke behind them. "Observing" is not such a passive thing as it sounds.

One of the Germans, who was simply a decoy, made back to his lines, while the other circled away into ours. A lot of anti-aircraft shells finally greeted him and he headed back our way. While this had been going on, "Red" Griffin, one of our Irish sergeants, who had been a Pittsburgh fireman, fitted a pan on his *Chauchat* automatic rifle, and when the German passed over us going back, he ran out from under the trees firing a stream of bullets until the pan was empty. "Red" was so much in earnest about it that the generals, who saw the whole performance, laughed. The plane, of course, was not touched. I never saw one brought down, but ran across the wrecks of a few here and there. Some were our own. The Germans had conducted this raid skillfully, and we were minus one balloon, while theirs continued to peer at us. Luckily they were short of artillery.

The rumor was passed around that afternoon that we were going back, and about five o'clock the word came that the barrage had made "Fritz" move on again, so that our "lost" battalions were able to leave their difficult positions in the Bois de la Fère. They had been relieved by other troops. That we were to have a rendezvous with the rest of the regiment in a rest billet to the rear was the rumor's golden lure.

At any rate our supper was cut short, as usual, by an order to move "right away." So I fed the men, while the captain hung around uneasily, not wanting to stint the men but between the "deil and the deep," as he was afraid of being caught unprepared. In a couple of hours we moved. Courpoil had been an interesting experience.

CHAPTER X

A REST IN THE WOODS

WE marched back from Courpoil the same way we had come, as far as Epieds. Our friend, the shredded German, was still holding on to his helmet. I understood what "holding on like grim death" meant when I looked at him.

At Epieds there was an immense jam of truck trains. Our own coming east were laden, while empty French *camions* were going back to the rail-head at Château-Thierry. We halted to let them pass and almost lost connection with the rest of the

battalion. I kept slipping a man between the moving
trucks every now and then until the first platoons
were all deployed as connecting files. When the
trucks finally did get by, we saw our two platoons
strung out in Indian file for hundreds of yards down
the road, which distance we made up by marching
when the rest of the battalion rested at the next halt.

Later on, we halted for a rest in front of a farmhouse with several outbuildings and a court. Here
some French wagoners were turning in to stay for
the night. Curiously enough, there were a woman
and some children here—the first we had seen in
a long while. We remembered this place as a wagon
nearly ran over Captain Law, thus (nearly) "immor-
talizing" him.

The French drivers were absolutely regardless of
infantry, and cut right across a column wherever
they could. One of them tried this as he turned in
at right angles across our path, in order to drive into
the little farmyard. The wagon wheels passed so
close to the captain that they brushed his boots.
This made him mad as a hornet. So when the next
wagon swung in, quite as ruthlessly as the other,
he raised his cane and gave the horses a cut that
made them rear back. There was a terrible jab-
bering in French and a jarring and creaking of
brakes all down the line. One Frenchman, who
shouted something at the captain, was pulled down
off his wagon by one of our men and given a swift

kick. The other Frenchmen gave him the laugh and the whole thing blew over in friendly bantering. Both our men and the *poilus* were too good-natured really to make trouble. There was one war on already.

Towards dark we marched through a hamlet with thatched roofs. It lay in a deep, little valley where two streams met. The mud was terrific. Trucks were mired here and there, and our shoes sucked and squelched as we passed through. Some artillery outfit had already appropriated the houses. "Our woods" lay just up the hill, rather decent ones. There were some old German dugouts in them, with the usual tangle of Boche telephone wire about, but the place was pretty clean. We were soon hidden for the night in the usual manner. But we did not dig in. We pitched our pup tents, being far enough behind the lines here to feel pretty safe. Despite that, some one ran across some old gas and there was a tremendous alarm that night. So many trucks and machine gun Fords being about, the effect was more than usually successful.

Next morning we moved out of this particular *bois* into another patch about a mile away. It seems that the woods we had occupied were supposed to be occupied by the 112th Infantry instead of by our own regiment. What difference it made, God only knows. Anyway, several thousand men moved, one regiment passing the other to the tune of much chaff. In a few hours we were all encamped again. Little paths cut through the woods. Along these the men sat in the doors of their tents cleaning their rifles as there had been some oil doled out. Oil was a scarce article. At first you could beg it from the truck drivers, but very soon they hardened their hearts, and rifles rusted away gaily. Then would come a great clean-up day.

Nick put my tent just on the edge of the woods, not far from the cooker. We were able to have an open fire here. A lot of my "friends" came around for supper. The French sergeant major brought me some wine, from where I do not presume to know, but there was a good time, stories, firelight and tobacco. This was the only camp-fire I saw in France from that time until after the Armistice.

In the field, under a few trees, was a battery of 75's almost at a forty-five degree angle, which told of the extreme range at which they were firing. They made sleep impossible. We always "rested" next to a battery of artillery. I spent the night working on some verse, as the rare chance of being alone and using a candle was not to be neglected. To keep the glow from showing through the tent I threw a blanket or two over it. By two o'clock I could stand the blasting and howls of the shells no longer, so I got up and went over to the battery.

It was in charge of a second lieutenant, a humorous Kentucky lad, who was getting his firing data over the telephone. The guns were firing at extreme range and using their heaviest charge. The flash leaped high above the treetops, and the gun recoiled and slid back into place like a piston rather than a cannon. The shocks of explosion were like blundering into some one on the street. It numbed my ear, yet the artillery lieutenant was talking over the telephone.

In an interval of firing I asked him if he happened to know what he was firing at. He showed me the map. The targets were mostly crossroads and villages. Just then some more data came over the wire.

"What is that?" he asked; then he gave some orders.

The men readjusted the gun and changed the charge. I think they put in a new gas ring and pads.

"Watch," said the lieutenant. "This is for an ammunition dump." He pointed toward the eastern horizon.

Then they fired—nothing happened.

Some further slight changes were made and again came the explosion. As the shriek of the shell died away, a great flower-pot of crimson light shot up into the sky over the horizon. That was the German ammunition dump.

You must imagine some crossroads in the woods over in the German lines with a lot of big shells going off, nitrose powder burning furiously, and darkness finally settling down over some blackened fragments of what had once been men.

Toward the Flame

All the roads to the rear of the German lines were at that time crowded with men and wagon trains. The scenes on those choked lines of retreat, as our shells burst on their withdrawing columns, must have been truly infernal. Over the edge of the world, uttering their banshee wails like screams of vengeance, and roaring like express trains, came the messengers of the outraged republics. There would be a frightful red flare, the bellow of an explosion, arms, legs, trunks of men, death-dealing fragments of jagged steel and whirling wreckage falling for miles along the gray-helmeted, rearward-plodding columns.* No use to cry *"Kamarad"* or shriek to *Gott.* It must have been during those nights of horror when our shells ate him up like cannibalistic devils that "Fritz" at last came to realize that "the jig was up."

It rained next day, so all the low-lying fields and roads were turned into a sea of sticky mud. The men stayed pretty close in their tents, wrapping themselves in their blankets along with their rifles, and only coming out for mess.

Rumors of a Y.M.C.A. canteen over at the little village drew me out in the afternoon. I tramped past the battery, silent now and out of range, and slipped and slithered into the village, where in a cowshed the Y.M.C.A. man was selling cigarettes, choco-

* Some German officers, prisoners, I talked to afterwards, spoke feelingly of the frightful scenes along the roads during the withdrawal from the Marne salient.

lates, and little cakes and butter biscuits. There was a long, helmeted line waiting patiently in the rain. Officers were constantly thrusting themselves in, and would take an unconscionable time choosing some particular brand of cigarette and demanding change while the rest of the line waited in the drizzle and manure-soaked water. It was one of the few privileges an officer had left to abuse.

One could look across the fields and see the men coming out of the woods in all directions, dragging their way across the heavy mud like brown flies over fly paper. There were a few trucks here, mired, and running their engines at a frightful rate, slipping and sloshing, with blue smoke rolling out from behind, and a deluge of water and mud flying off their vainly whirling wheels. Hell is not paved with good intentions but with mud.

This was one of the few places where the whole regiment got together: the whole brigade in fact. The colonel had his car and the headquarters company near him, bivouacked in a little cove in the woods. One got an impression of lines of Ford cars with their radiators all staring at one, for the machine gun company with its trucks was here too. Then there was the equipment of the one-pound cannon section, and the trench-mortar platoon lying around, tripods, and little carts and chests, and perhaps a tent here and there with clerks, and a typewriter clicking in it. There were orderlies with red armbands, and those privileged characters of the regiment, the colonel's chauffeur and striker, the regimental sergeant major, the intelligence officer, and the statistical officer, ready to ask about that overdue paper work. One generally met the chaplain here, too, a kindly, lovable man, much saddened by things he had seen, and destined to make the last sacrifice later on.

Such was headquarters.

Wyke and I went to pay a visit to Lieutenant Fletcher, the scout officer of the third battalion, whom I had met at Courpoil, searching for his outfit. I describe him because he was the kind of man whose essential strength of personality stood out clearly. In all that mud and confusion, he was living under a wagon, clean, clear-cut of feature, merry and wise, with a few good books around him, and something succinct and amusing to say.

Fletcher was always commenting on things. Under the wagon he was dry and clean, and that was typical. No mud of any kind ever touched him. All the filth and littlenesses of that vast experience of war passed him by like the unremembered faces on the street. Only its vastness, its youthful vigor, and its sacrifices were real to him. Yet he was a better man physically than most; a fast runner, a good shot, handsome, a keen thinker, deeply conscientious, with a broad sense of humor and a catching laugh. He should have lived to have children instead of being snuffed out later on in a miserable garret in Fismes by a chance shell.

I went to pay him twenty francs I owed him and to hear what he had to say. Wyke and I sat around while his striker brought us something to eat, coffee in big canteen cups, and white, bursting, boiled potatoes in jackets. Fletcher waved his hands about majestically and ironically quoted the *Rubáiyát*. It seemed like spreading a Persian carpet in the woods. We all laughed with Omar, taking his advice about the wine literally, and applying it. Fletcher had a canteenful hanging under the wagon.

Another night of wind and rain was followed by a sultry morning. The fields steamed while we waited for another regiment to move out ahead of us. The "rest" was over. We had hoped to get back to a real town to refit, such had been the wishful rumor, but it was many a weary day before that came true, months in fact.

CHAPTER XI

A GRAVE IN THE WOODS

SO much of our time at the front was spent in marching and then lying around in the woods that to recount it in detail would only give its main impression, one of tiresome monotony.

That day we passed a German airplane shot down in a field. At a halt, a lot of the men ran over to see it, and I remember feeling too weak to stop them. We moved on again up a corduroy road through the woods, which the enemy was "sniping" with an Austrian 77. These guns shot on a very flat trajectory and there was no time to dodge. The report of the cannon and the report of the shell came almost together. "Bang-crash, bang-crash." There were both German and American dead along here, as the fight had just passed that way. We were following up in reserve, and it was said the infantry was "hung up" some miles ahead. The big noise we heard was going on about Croix Rouge Farm, still held by the enemy.

We had a long wait in a field where something interesting happened. "Fritz's" planes had been coming over without let or hindrance all day, observing the roads, and switching their artillery on them. I went over to a little farm to hunt water during this halt, where I found a French anti-aircraft battery had just moved in. The men were sitting around loafing, cooking, and sleeping. The officers were settling themselves in some of the vacant rooms. Suddenly a whistle blew. Such a change you never saw. Instantly, all was business. A German plane was coming over pretty high and taking its time. Suddenly the whole air went to pieces about it. The French shells broke so near, it had to drop, make a swoop, and turn tail. It was followed for a long way by a trail of bursting shells like white powder puffs, and the French shooting was good. I remember hearing the pieces from the shells landing a long time afterwards in the woods.

The next stage of our journey was a macadam-

ized road with the German arbor camouflage along
one side, with signs and painted canvas across it like
the "Welcome Home" signs of old home week. But
these signs said it was *"verboten"* for more than four
wagons at a time to be on any given section of road,
and also blazed forth the information, "This road
can be seen by your enemies."

At one place there was an unharmed and charming little villa, quite Japanese in its effect, whose
entire fenced-in garden made a well-kept German
cemetery with many rows of new crosses and mounds.
Here and there was a helmet on top of a grave. The
wounded were coming back along this road, and
some prisoners. One could look along it for miles,
the ambulances racing down its length, men passing
this way and that, ammunition carts, automobiles and
side cars. It was quite like a busy park street on a
fine day, only there was a different spirit here, where
every one was bound on the same errand, for there
was news of hot fighting ahead.

By evening, however, the firing had stopped, and
our lieutenant colonel met us and led us into another woods, a grassy open one this time, with the
usual artillery near by. The Germans had been logging here, and had marked all the best trees with a
ring of green paint. Graves, helmets and old machine
guns' débris were scattered through the tract. Here
we stayed for four or five days pretty comfortably.
Another division, the 32nd U. S., moved in near by.

A Grave in the Woods

I had a bed in a deep ditch at this place, covered with logs, stones, and boughs. The men lived in holes which they kept digging a little deeper every day. We heard a few shells fall in answer to our batteries, but none very near us. News of the fighting came back from the other infantry brigade in our division. We saw wounded and prisoners whenever we went out on the main road. A sergeant of another regiment told me that in one place the Germans arrived on a train and got off almost in our lines— where they were immediately taken prisoners. They did not know we had moved up so far. After all, there was nothing in the landscape to mark where "Hunland" began.

The fighting eventually moved entirely out of our ken, and we went into pup tents.

An order for several hours' drill a day now came around. The men were not permitted to rest but were taken out and bored by old training camp stuff. I was surprised how patient they were.

Dysentery began to show up here due to the bad water we were forced to drink. Some of the men were absolutely prostrated and the condition of the woods became bad, flies among other things. We had some bad beans for supper one night that nearly floored Lieutenant Glendenning and me. We were both ghastly sick, and slept until about noon the next day, waking up in a hot, sunny tent with flies buzzing, both so weak and pale around the gills that we laughed at each other. Memoranda had been sent around warning us that the Germans had poisoned wells and springs. Our water carts sometimes went miles for good water, but it was impossible not to catch something sooner or later with the vast deal of decay going on.

At that place I saw a very curious thing, a luminous grave. A horse or mule had been buried hastily, probably by the Germans, and quite near the surface. You could see the barrel-like outline of the ribs. One night I noticed, as I looked out of the tent into the dark woods, something glowing faintly. It was the grave. I called the attention of several of the men to it and they distinctly saw it, too.

To give a diary of our life here would be uninteresting. The last two days the guns moved in and shot right over our heads. I felt the ground shaking all night. From here, however, I did make an interesting trip.

I had some personal business to accomplish with the division paymaster and got the colonel's permission to visit division headquarters, then supposed to be in a little hamlet only a few miles distant. I passed brigade headquarters now ensconced in the little villa with the cemetery in its garden. There was some wash drying on some of the crosses, and several automobiles and motorcycles drawn up before the gate. A staff conference of some kind, I suppose.

Walking down to the little village, I found that division headquarters had moved that morning back to a little town just up the Marne from Château-Thierry, then about fifteen kilometers away. However, I determined to catch a truck and make the trip.

The roads in the rear of the armies were like a great boulevard. All the corners were well placarded, and the military police were on duty directing traffic. Trucks, limousines, Fords, the horse-drawn French wagons, and fast *camions,* artillery with huge tractors, and bodies of men were going both ways in a constant stream. Now and then an ambulance hurtled by, going like lightning, and one would get a glimpse of the feet of men lying on stretchers, or pale bandaged fellows, arms in slings or heads bound up, sitting and swaying on the seats, with the surgeon in the front seat beside the chauffeur. Then there were endless strings of trucks in trains, moving along steadily all at the same pace, a limousine car at the head with the motor transport officer inside wearing his Sam Browne belt, like a dandy in a glass case. The truck drivers were provided with rifles in a leather sling, as were the side cars, little tin bath-tubs on wheels that flashed by constantly.

Toward the Flame

Trucks would pick one up, and it was possible to ride for miles and get back the same day. One of the military policemen flagged a truck for me, and we sped down over the white road toward the Marne, with troops camped on either side. The road turned at Dormans, to which there was a long descent.

This town stands directly on the Marne. There had been a terrific fight there a few weeks before. It certainly showed it. Despite this, our men were living in the houses, and the place had a busy aspect, but there was no glass in the windows, few roofs, and nothing but soldiers about. In the folds of the ground up the high hillside, batteries of artillery were camped. We stopped here and filled our radiator from a garden well.

Once out of Dormans, we fairly raced down the level road along the Marne, passing through the villages whose names had been made suddenly famous during the battle along the river; then on through Gland with its ruined church, across from which was the garden where I had met my friend a few nights before. I wondered where he was now. The place looked different by daylight, and there was another outfit billeted there.

Gland was as far as the truck went, so I got out and was planning my next move when I met Colonel Pucey of the division staff who had a car waiting. He told me he would take me to division headquarters. But first, he said, he had to go over to the other side of the Marne with another colonel, as they were trying to locate a place to park the ammunition trains that were coming up from the base at Meaux. I was only too pleased at the chance to go with him.

We had some little difficulty in finding a bridge over the Marne, but finally crossed over on a pontoon structure near Chézy. It was intensely interesting to see this country where we had been facing the enemy a few weeks before. Chézy was just a little way from Crézancy and those woods which the men had called "Death Valley," where so many of them had been killed by shell fire.

All the intensity and mystery that the presence of the enemy lends to a place had gone. The towns were full of our troops, the roads crowded with truck trains, and every wood the parking place for ammunition and ration trains. We ran up to Fossoy, which had been the headquarters of the 7th Infantry, crossing our old friend, the Paris Aqueduct, with some difficulty, and running along it for a piece. Graves were everywhere.

The French refugees were beginning to come back. On one of the roads I saw a cart, a high-wheeled cart, with a fat, little, dappled-gray horse plodding along toward the Marne with an old French peasant in blue blouse and wooden shoes driving, his grey-haired wife holding on and dusting along beside him. The French soldiers were reaping in some of the fields, a harvest of a different sort than had been reaped there a few days before. High up on the plateau back of the Marne, near where we had been billeted in June, we met some of the officers of the ammunition train for whom we had been looking. The two automobiles were stopped and in a short time both colonels settled on the woods where it was to be parked.

Great care had to be exercised in such matters. If a rain came on, mud might make it impossible for the trucks to get out of the place where they were parked, and consequent delay in bringing ammunition up to the front in a crisis might result. There was rifle ammunition at this place, packed in bandoliers in neat wooden boxes with a tin case receptacle inside.

The business of parking once settled, we fairly tore down to Château-Thierry, which was the railhead at that time. And railheads were liable to be bombed. As we came down the hill near the town an airplane came swooping along the road. The colonel ordered the car drawn up under a tree and said to the other colonel, "Shall we get out, John?" John did not reply. I stuck my head out of the window and saw the red, white and blue circles and enjoyed the "situation." It was one of our own planes.

The roads leading into the town were tremendously congested. They had the railroad working, and we waited at the crossing by a mill whose iron roof was a lacework of bullet holes, while train after train went by; flat cars with guns blocked to the floor and peering up at an angle at the sky, cattle cars with horses looking out, a wisp of hay in their teeth, and cattle cars full of men, the famous *"40 hommes, 8 chevaux."* The men had their shirts off; it was hot and their feet were dangling over the edge, or they were sitting or standing in groups by the door. Old passenger cars bumped past, some compartments empty with perhaps a smashed door, and others full of harassed and tired-looking officers, their musette bags and pistols hanging from the racks, and the tassels and upholstering of the seats appearing indescribably tawdry with big boots resting on them, while the remains of food and tobacco was scattered about. The trains backed and shifted with whoops and coughs.

Meanwhile the motor trucks and side cars "inched up" and stood beating and pulsing in rows until there was an opening across the tracks. Then the whole

mess poured like a flood over the railroad and into the town. We had some difficulty in finding the right bridge to cross over. The French guard stopped us at one, but at the other, another pontoon structure, there was no difficulty.

I was impressed to see how quickly Château-Thierry was reviving. Already a few women and children had returned. Despite the shell craters and wreckage, it already looked like a habitable town. In such a place division headquarters had no difficulty in making themselves comfortable. They were billeted in one of the suburbs. The different messes each had a house to themselves, and after my home in the ditch up in the woods, they looked very comfortable, with chairs and furniture, a set table, and orderlies, and nicely made-up cots. Officers were sitting around in gardens, talking and smoking, for it was near dinner time. It looked almost peaceful. Under it all, though, pulsed the steady throb and rumble of the trucks and the clatter of the boards on the pontoon bridge, the throb of the motor transport, which was indeed the heartbeat of the army.

I quickly transacted my business and came out of the town hall, where the offices were, into the glow of a beautiful sunset, just in time to catch a captain of engineers, the supply officer of his regiment, who was going back to the lines in his dusty limousine filled with cartons of cigarettes, chocolates, and cakes, plunder from the Y.M.C.A. and Red Cross. Such articles were always welcome at the front where supplies were few and far between.

He dropped me at a little town on a crossroads near my own regiment. And after a few minutes' walk I found "our woods" with the men sitting around in the twilight, talking, smoking or gambling in excited groups, whence came invocations to Fortune and the snapping of fingers, while the dice rolled out on the blankets. Nick had saved me some supper piping hot in my mess pan, and I fell to, feeling mentally and bodily refreshed by my little trip. What a bright sun, what white towns along how blue a river! The guns were silent that night and we slept.

CHAPTER XII

ANOTHER NIGHT MARCH

I THINK I mentioned that the Germans had marked all the best trees in this wood for logging. Many of them they had already cut down, and the huge logs, for they were very ancient oaks, lay scattered about here and there. Between two of these and under them, in a hole, the major had set up shop and every once in a while he or the adjutant would bob up like jacks-in-the-pulpit to bawl out an order or give directions, to the quiet amusement of all in the vicinity. In a curious way they lost much prestige by this behavior.

The Y.M.C.A. man attached to our regiment came and held his sale right in front of the major's quarters on a little rutted road. He would have a few cartons (called "cartoons" by the men) of cigarettes, or baskets full of small jellies put up in pasteboard cups, sometimes chocolates, boxes of cigars, and little cakes wrapped in wax paper. There was always a dense ring formed around him right away, and things were bought up like mad, the officers snatching off the cigars, and every one wanting to get more than his share. There was also much discontent at prices, and haggling over change, which was very difficult to make, the men's pay generally being in franc notes of large denominations. The harassed "Y" men were for the most part very patient, but the nature of their business, selling gum drops and cakes when civilization hung in the balance, was so petty that they were bound to be despised by the very men for whom they labored. All these things might have been issued as part of the rations from the ration dump or sold by accredited sutlers or a commissary agent. A religious organization that found its greatest field in purveying stationery, jelly, and ginger snaps behind the lines of battle merited the contempt which it so often received. As a matter of fact, there was little else it could do, and that in itself was a great comment.

Toward the Flame

It was here that we got the news of Fère-en-Tardenois: how our men had met the Prussian Guards in hand-to-hand fighting and worsted them, leaving the streets full of bayoneted dead. We also saw the great cloud in the sky when our aviators bombed the German dump there, a vast, mushroom-shaped column of black smoke that rushed up into the sky, and then curled out like an umbrella all white at the edges. That had been one of the main depots for the drive *"nach Paris."* There was a German bond issue in the umbrella-shaped cloud. About this time division headquarters sent around a memorandum telling how the roads back of the German lines were full of retreating troops singing, "We're going back to Germany," and it was here that the first really persistent rumor of an Austrian peace proffer began to be circulated. We saw the New York *Herald's* edition once in a while, but it was always many days old. Nevertheless, there was elation and victory in the air. Our fellows seemed to take this for granted, though, from the first. It was well for us that we had not met the Germans some years earlier.

In the training camps the British officers had taught the bayonet and both British and French trainers had instilled in us the idea of taking no prisoners. Aside from any other considerations, this was a stupid policy, and I think it was about this time that the major general directed in a memorandum that quarter be given, as otherwise the enemy resisted to the last, which cost us many unnecessary casualties. Our men could not, and hardly ever did, have the hatred for the Germans that the personnel of the other allied armies were said to have had. On the whole this was quite fortunate and encouraged the Germans to surrender more easily.*

We moved out after supper one night to the chorus of the guns, which had been silent for several days. They were firing at extreme range. I anticipated a long march and was not disappointed. Next to the march just after Château-Thierry, it was the hardest test so far, and it was all at night, too.

We passed a battle-scarred farm with long French guns folded down on their carriages in the fields close by, the personnel billeted in the farm buildings. The French officers I talked to here were much elated, and, I noted, looked on our men with great respect. One of them filled my canteen with wine, patting me on the back. It would be over soon. *"C'est fini maintenant!"* There were about twenty dead horses there in a row. "To-morrow," said the Frenchman,

---

* Several former officers in the English army and others, inform me that the idea of a personal hatred between the soldiers of the British and German forces was a convention of the propaganda of the war period. They say that, especially toward the last of the struggle, respect, and even a certain friendliness and mutual pity animated all concerned in the common misery. I can only add that no such idea was taught by the instructors sent to the United States by various foreign governments. The French taught war as a science, the British like football coaches; to the Americans war was a business enterprise on a national scale with life insurance, union wages and shower baths for the employees. Occasionally one met a genuine soldier lost amid regiments of employees.—H. A., 1934.

holding his nose and laughing. It seems they were *"German* horses!" I wondered if his resentment extended even to the mineral kingdom.

This was another wooded, rolling plateau we were entering upon. On and on, up and down, we marched, the road leading past woods and fields with a faint moon just showing—on through little ruined towns with lights glimmering through cracks here and there behind blanketed windows. There were halts for the major to examine maps, twists, and turns, and stops to let truck trains and automobiles by. Nothing is more tiresome than constantly starting and halting under heavy equipment. The men grumbled, and when it came on to drizzle, which it did gradually, they lit matches to light cigarettes and pipes, a dangerous thing in case of enemy planes being near.

About three o'clock we stumbled into a little village where the word was passed that there was to be an hour's halt. It was utterly and profoundly dark; a thick, wet, clammy dark with the rain falling steadily. We were ordered not to allow the men to go into the houses, but as it was impossible to see beyond your own hand, I knew that this could not be stopped since the men were standing right next to the open doors and windows of the buildings, built as usual right along the edge of the street. To expect them to lie down in the streaming road was too much. As a matter of fact, some of them did lie down in the road ditch, too insensible to care. I got some of the sergeants near me and climbed through a window myself into a little room where I flopped down in a corner. As I did so I noticed the faint outline of a man against the opposite window, but I went off into a doze right away without speaking to him.

For some reason the halt was shortened, and we moved in about twenty minutes instead of an hour. I heard the stir in the street and jumped up to go out, but remembering the man next to the window, I went over to wake him up. He was sitting in a chair and he did not move when I spoke. As I leaned forward to shake him, the peculiar shape of his helmet and a faint deathly odor told me the tale. It was a dead German.

Once in line, there was a long delay. Strange as it may seem, I did not go back into that room, but propped myself up in the window and went to sleep. We were all numb with fatigue. The men simply sat in the road helplessly. They were as wet as they could get. My trench coat kept me dry about the body, and my tin hat shed rain. Sitting dripping in the window, I had one of the most vivid dreams of home and carefree boyhood times that a man could have. It unnerved me so much that I really had no bark in my voice when it came to getting the men on their feet again. That was certainly one miserable night.

Another Night March

We scrambled on for about a hundred yards, and then halted again. Everybody made a rush for the houses this time. I got into a corner with Lieutenant Glendenning, where he slept. Tired as I was, I could not. Leaning up against me, Glen talked in his sleep. The room was jammed, men kept coming in and out, stepping on the sleepers. One fellow, a young lad, has a terrible cough that ended in a maddening gag and a wheeze. He began to cry out after a while, frightened by it. There was nothing to do for him. Some of the hopeless began telling putrid stories. At the first gray of the morning we moved, but several of the sleepers were left behind. It was impossible to wake them all, scattered as they were

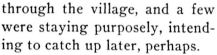

through the village, and a few were staying purposely, intending to catch up later, perhaps.

Deliberate straggling like this seemed the worst of crimes at this time. The captain was a pillar of strength on that march. Glen and I were tuckered out with dysentery and tottered along together.

I was in hopes that we were going to get a good woods or a village to billet in, but we had no such luck. We passed a lot of dead Germans in one place at the top of a hill. It looked as though there had not been much quarter given there. The road slithered two feet deep in mud down a hillside and onto a flat space, across which we could see some old German hangars and barracks. There was a narrow-gauge railway here with overthrown cars like an abandoned coal-mine working. At the bottom of the valley was a tremendous grange or farm, all knocked to pieces. We headed for this and I had hopes—but it was not to be.

As we expected, the order came, and we marched right out into the muddy wheat stubble. The men did not attempt to pitch shelter tents but just sat down, too fagged and indifferent to care. The kitchens were not in sight yet, and it was still raining. We sat and sat. After a while the sun came up. It seemed a useless proceeding on its part. I went down to the farm to try and wash up and scrub the dirt and mustard gas out of my fingers, which were painful with raw and festering hangnails. That farm, a huge place, was almost a perfect symbol of war.

The big sheds outside were full of cases of potato-masher bombs and all manner of curious signal-light material left by the Germans. The ground around the great, square, brick building had been trampled into a welter of mud. Inside the courtyard a thick cast-iron spigot with its handle broken off was running constantly, making pools all over the place. French soldiers were slushing back and forth, cooking, or asleep in the rooms that opened onto the court. Part of the upper story had been shot away. Giant chimneys and staring windows looked at one from the roofless rooms, filled with a devil's medley of charred tables, broken china, old clothes and weapons. There was a hot, fetid breath from the stables, where the French had too many horses crowded into filthy stalls, and a plague of flies crawled over everything, making sleep impossible and eating nauseous. This farm must have been a well-run plant at one time. There was an engine room with wheels and shafts twisted into a writhing mass by the flames, and a water tank riddled by bullets. Over everything was a glistening film of black sewer-like mud, mingled with plaster dust, fragments of red roof tiles, horse manure, and broken furniture. Despite all of this, though, it was better than the lake of mud in the fields.

Nick got the solid alcohol, heated a can of salmon he had been carrying, and some French "monkey meat." With this and some hard-tack we made a meal. We got a corner in the stable, drew the blankets over our faces to keep off the flies, and went to sleep. When I got up, the sun had come out strong and the men were putting up their pup tents in the fields. But best of all, the kitchens had come. I had my shelter tent put up close to our cooker.

While I was eating mess I noticed a square lead plate that the cooks were using to set things on.

Another Night March

The mess sergeant told me they had picked it up at Château-Thierry in one of the houses—"where there was a row on the wall." On turning it over I found it to be a lead plaque with very excellent Italian renaissance figures depicting the most frankly pornographic scene I ever looked at. I was so tired that I remember the antique exuberance of the thing struck me as being incredible. It had, however, the unusual merit of being too heavy to carry around, which is more than similar modern postcards possess.

We soon moved again, in the rain, to a woods overlooking a valley in which there was a balloon company and two or three machine guns posted to keep off the enemy's planes. The woods were filled with artillery here. At our next move—we were being held in reserve while an attack went on some miles away—the barrage was weirdly magnificent.

There was no longer any pretense of hiding the guns; they simply stood out in fields or at the edge of woods; and that night the "display" was unusually intense. The Germans were making a stand on the Vesle, a few kilometers away. When the drumfire was at its height there was one wood that seemed to be a grove of lightnings with a constant seething flame along its front, and everywhere through the meadows great jets and tongues of fire cut the darkness like knife stabs. The officers gathered into a little hushed group and watched it. After the thunder ceased suddenly, the silence seemed strange.

Toward the Flame

That night saw us in another woods, always nearer the Vesle River. I slept under a French wagon with the top sergeant. Peeping in the body of it at first, we dislodged some of the canvas on top, and a lot of water that had collected in one of the folds ran down onto the sleeping French inside. There was considerable hard feeling for a while, which died away in snores. On the ground it was cold. The men slept huddled together in their slickers.

We were joined next day by three lieutenants from the 77th Division, which accession helped out considerably, as our company was short of officers. They were all fine fellows, anxious to do their share, and more. Here it was, too, that we saw the end of the observation balloon that now lay behind us.

About four o'clock one afternoon a German plane came over and shot it down in a whirl of flame and smoke. The observer escaped by the parachute, and the enemy headed back straight for home, heedless of the jabber of machine guns and the popping of a million rifles. There was great indignation. It seemed too easy. That night we made the distance clear to the Vesle, a memorable march for us.

CHAPTER XIII

THE MARCH TO THE VESLE, AND FISMES

BY THE flickering light of the cannon on a hundred hills, we started on our march to the Vesle. We were fast catching up with the battle line now as the Germans had halted on the river, and as we advanced over the plateau, winding down into the valleys, and across the hills, we began gradually to get into the shelled area again.

At one place the road descended into a steep ravine and made a sudden turn, where under a rocky ledge there was an immense cavern capable of holding, it was said, an entire battalion. In the dark of the night it was a strange thing to look back into its recesses and see the lanterns and lights moving as if in a subterranean world. Of course, in there, they were free from all observation. There were also a good many ambulances and trucks coming and going, and the place seemed to be used for a general storehouse.

As we came up out of the valley, we saw a flat plain beyond, and in the distance, lighting up a line of black woods for an instant, I saw the unwelcome wink of a falling shell. Away off over the hills some German flares went up. We were getting close again!

That whole flat was saturated with gas. By this time, however, we had learned not to put our masks on until the order came. One or two places the gas was choking, then on another little rise it would clear up again. Everything went well until we came to a crossroads, which the enemy was evidently gunning for, as several gas shells fell very close by in the fields with their characteristic "flop."

A few seconds later the gas was so strong there was no need for an order. Every one shouted, "gas!" and put on his mask, with the usual result of great trouble. Platoons and companies lost touch with each another, and there was great difficulty in giving orders or having them understood.

As a matter of fact, there was no real need of a mask even after the shells fell, as I left mine off, and so did several of the other officers, without any ill effects except a little choking sensation at the time. One sad thing did happen that night, however.

A big high explosive shell came over so close to us we felt sure from its sound it was going to burst very near. There is nothing worse than listening to the increasing howl of a shell and realizing that *this* time it really is going to burst near you. How near? That is the vital question. This particular shell burst several hundred yards away, tearing through the trees and crashing with a red flash that lit up the road and the columns of troops. Then we heard those awful agonized screams and cries for help that so often followed. It is impossible to make people at home understand what listening to them does to your brain. You can never get rid of them again.

What had happened was this: the big chap who rode the horses on our company kitchen had been caught in the burst and mortally hurt. Every bit of flesh from his waist down had been blown off his legs and yet he lived for some time. The splendid big grays were killed. I heard about all this next day.

Very late that night we camped in a field for some hours. It was the coldest weather we had felt and I slept little, trying in vain to keep my feet and legs covered, and wondering what it would be like in

January if we was cold in August. As day began
to break, the captain and I moved the men over into
a trench along a road that disappeared over the edge
of the hill about two hundred yards away. The
"trench" was simply the road ditch dug deeper and
full of man-holes. I found a pit in it with a fine piece
of sheet iron for a roof. To judge by the star shells,
there was only a half mile or so of valley between us
and the enemy. At daybreak, to our left, we saw the
gaunt skeleton of a shelled church with a cluster of
ruined houses around it. This was Mont Saint-
Martin, according to the map. And in the valley,
just over the slope of the hill, lay Fismes.

We were almost on the verge of that slope and
overlooked quite an amphitheater of hills behind us.
In front there was a field, a stretch of a few hundred
yards, and then the ground fell away steeply to the
Vesle. From our trench as far as I could see the
road was lined on both sides with bobbing "tin hats."
Here are some notes I took at the time showing
exactly how it appeared.

"I can look down the trench from here and see
a dirty mess pan crawling with flies, and a fat rusty
canteen attached to a belt. An old helmet, like a
hurt turtle on the parapet, is dragging a chin strap
tied to a bloody rag, and the eye of a machine gun
stares at me from its tripod in perpetual surprise.
There are alternate bands of shadow and white sunlight across the trench, and down its long vista I see

many men in a row. A fat soldier is sleeping with his back in the air like a pile of clothes, another, in profile, is staring across the fields, and the feet of a dead man stick out stiffly over a stretcher. His hands are raised to his gas mask in rigid protest, where there is blood. There is a blank air of utter idleness about. It is a lonesome land full of the sense of impending disaster."

All that day we lay along the road and heard machine gun fire and trench mortars from Fismes in the valley. There was a constant harassing artillery fire, too, from both sides. Our position was under direct observation, and every once in a while "Fritz" would skip a few shells over the fields at the working parties or grub details that passed constantly up and down the road. Every now and then a man was carried by on a stretcher, limp and gassed. They were bringing them up out of the valley all day long. Such groups were always the purveyors of "news." Wounded men were eagerly questioned, but very

few lucid accounts could be gotten. Naturally enough, each man knew only how the fight went at his own little corner.

Ambulances tore back and forth, for which the enemy gunned regularly. The doctors and drivers showed great skill in braving one stretch of road in particular. Just as they came up over the brow of the hill out of the valley, there was a place where they were in full view of the other side of the river. Then there was a little dip, a swale of ground, down which the cars came hurtling at full speed. The Germans calculated on this, and they would drop a shell a little in advance down the road, and exactly into the little hollow, hoping the car would run into it. There were some breathless escapes. One fellow, I remember, stopped just on the brow of the hill, let the shell burst ahead of him, and then tore down the road, leaning out to shout as he swooped past, "——— them that time!" It took cool nerve to do that.

Another exhibition of German gunnery took place later on in the day. Most of our rolling kitchens had been left near the cave we had passed the night before. But those belonging to the outfits fighting in Fismes were kept hidden in the woods above the town, whence from time to time one would try to get down near enough for the mess details to come up to meet it and carry down a hot meal.* To do

* As a great deal has been said in this narrative about cookers, eating, etc., it may not be out of place to remark here that only the soldiers of romances are strong enough nobly to do without food.

that, the cookers very often had to expose themselves, as the whole slope of the plateau could be seen by the enemy.

I saw a kitchen come down a road, driving very fast, and smoking like a fire-engine. Just as it got near a big tree, a shell burst in front of it. They tried to turn around, but luckily did not succeed as another shell fell right behind them. By this time the horses were frantic and tore off through the fields with the mess sergeant and his men taking after them. This was the safest thing they could do, for in the fields they were comparatively safe. Several bodies of men coming down this same road were also scattered.

Sitting on the hill and observing all this as a spectator, I could not help but think that much loss might have been avoided by cutting across fields oftener. Men are so prone to follow a beaten path that they would almost rather be killed on it than take a new one. "Whither thou goest, I will go," seems to be written on the heart of the average soldier. Seeing how all the roads were covered by German artillery, I remembered this Scripture against a future time.

Our kitchen came up about four o'clock, but stayed back a little way in a grove and out of sight. We had to carry the meal about a mile in the clumsy receptacles provided, because we could not risk (after the tragedy of the night before) drawing shells and thus perhaps losing more men and horses. This was the first meal we had eaten for about twenty-four hours, so it went well. It was the last hot meal we got for many a day. I sent some of it over to the captain of "A" company, who was sitting with one of his lieutenants just across the road looking rather hungry. His kitchen had not yet appeared. Little incidents like this were remembered, as the captain was badly wounded and the lieutenant killed a day or so later. They were very gay then, although I knew both of them were ill.

Meals were carried from the rolling kitchens by sticking a pole through the handle of the cook pans, or pouring the food into large galvanized receptacles like milk cans with handles. No convenient vessels were provided for our mess details, who had to carry unwieldy and heavy contrivances, often slushing out half of the contents en route and forced to make slow going under fire. Our splendid system of supply broke down at the last link, in carrying the food from the kitchens to the lines. To be in the front line in the American Army at that time was to go hungry. Vessels that could have been swung on hooks from poles, tanks to be strapped to the back, anything would have been better than what we had, and the large number of men necessary on a mess detail to carry a hot meal increased the chance of casualties manifold.*

Late that afternoon we were issued rockets of

* Such articles were supplied later on in the war.

different kinds for signals, so that it was not difficult to prognosticate a move. Nevertheless, at dark all the men crawled into their holes and went to sleep. I remember feeling quite snug under my iron roof when a slight rain came on.

The time was now at hand when we were to look back on that quiet trench as a place of luxury and ease.

CHAPTER XIV

INTO THE PIT

LATE that night the captain wakened me and told me to get the company ready, as we were going to move. The platoon leaders went down the trench, wakening the men with the help of the sergeants, and in a few moments the dark masses of the platoons could be dimly made out standing on the gleaming white road. Each platoon was provided with its own rockets, which, for the most part, none of us had the slightest idea how to use. No instruction was provided. That a red rocket was at

that time the call for a barrage was the extent of
our knowledge. It was pitch black, but in the velvet
darkness the battalion began to move down the hill
toward Fismes.

The road fell away quite rapidly from the plateau
with a high bank on our left, screening us from the
Germans and the valley, on the far side of which
they lay. There were shelter holes and dugouts in
places along the bank, but at the bottom we emerged
into a deep side valley with a railroad track. A
stream ran down this through Fismes and emptied
into the Vesle beyond. The town itself lay on the
flat between the hills and the river.

As we emerged onto the flat, we could look back
at the heights and see the machine guns spitting fire
from the woods at the Germans on the other side of
the river. There were shots coming back too. At
one place, just off the road in a wood, the enemy's
shells had fallen into the ammunition dump of our
machine guns, and the ammunition was burning
fiercely, making a bright glow and exploding like a
lot of firecrackers. I think we must have been observed as we passed this fire, for they started to shell
the road so as to make it very lively. Just at the foot
of the hill, where the little stream flowed into the
Vesle and emerged onto a flat, our engineers were
repairing a bridge. "Fritz" had been gunning steadily for this, arousing with each shell a violent chattering from the nests of machine guns on our side

of the valley. The engineers had not yet finished repairing the bridge, so there was only a narrow footpath over it as yet, and here the battalion halted in the dark. The major turned aside into a roofless ruin for a while. The whole place was redolent of gas.

By the light of the burning ammunition I saw a man's legs lying by the road, buttocks up. The whole upper part of the body had been taken off by a shell, and the two naked legs looked exactly like a giant frog's. Things started to happen here. I was talking to Charley Wright, the company artificer, when a spent rifle bullet hit him on the helmet right above the eyes. It glanced off after tearing the front

rim from his helmet, and then bounced off mine. Just then the enemy started gunning for the woods in dead earnest.

A large number of shells passed right over our heads and b u r s t immediately beyond—a few yards lower, and they would have cleaned the highway. Everybody at first lay flat. We crawled forward a few yards and gained the shelter of some stone piles and logs just off the road. The gas seemed like a fog, and we put on our masks. I lay there for several minutes. The explosion and red glare were terrific, but after a while I saw that no shells fell on the road. Taking heart at this, Sergeant Griffin and I got up and ran along it for a short distance. Small pieces of iron fragments rattled off us several times. A little way along the road I met Lieutenant Horner of "C" company.

"We must tell the major we can't lie here," I shouted.

"We're supposed to go into Fismes and relieve the 112th Infantry," he replied. This was the first time I had heard what our mission was.

I told the captain I would go ahead and try to find our way and some shelter. None of us had any idea

203

what lay on the other side of the little bridge. I ran along the road with Sergeant Griffin and found Lieutenant Horner again, who said he would go with us, so we headed for the bridge.

I must say that road was terrific. Four or five shells a minute were coming. There was always one in the air. These burst with an earth-rocking smash on the other side of the road, just on the far side of the railway embankment. On the "safe" side of the road were the prone figures of the men hugging the ground. Branches, stones, iron fragments, and all manner of débris was hurtling about us; trees were crashing, and over our heads the machine guns were firing in a frenzy of chattering rage.

We found the engineers working frantically at their bridge, an old stone approach that they were trying to repair with planks. I questioned the engineer officer in a series of shouts, and he gave us a guide to take us to the dugout of the major of the 112th, whose battalion was occupying the town. We crossed the bridge on one plank, which was all that was ready, and found ourselves immediately among the houses and on the paved street of a good-sized town.

Behind us was the pandemonium of the barrage and the hammers of the engineers working feverishly at the bridge, all of which echoed up the empty street, mingled with the crackle of roof slates, and the tiles and bricks over which we stumbled. Pressing on for about two blocks, we turned suddenly into the main street of the town.

The fronts of large and handsome houses, built wall to wall, looked blindly across at each other with rows of open doors and yawning windows, as far as the eye could reach. It was a city of the dead, only wakened by the noise of firing, the glare of strange lights, and the flicks of rifle fire here and there.

At our backs the street ran out into the country onto the usual white tree-lined road, down which, a few hundred yards beyond, a furious rifle fight was in progress. Some of our men were sniping diligently from a house near by. There were strange lulls at times when an appalling silence would settle down over everything.

We turned up another side street. At a place where it cut through a little hill between two walls of rock, the guide turned aside. Lifting up a blanket that revealed a gleam of light, we entered what had once been a big wine cellar, a cave in the rock, now being used as a command post dugout. By the yellow light of several guttering candles and a carefully shaded lantern a group of officers were dozing about a table on which lay a map and the remnants of a meal. Back in the shadows could be dimly seen the forms of the sleeping runners and scouts who were always so numerous at any headquarters. Everybody, of course, who had the slightest excuse, and some slackers, invariably crowded into such a place of safety. Among the crowd of runners and orderlies it was indeed hard to separate the sheep from the goats. Consequently the air in there was fetid, and so tainted with gas that everybody felt drowsy.

I reported myself to a captain of the 112th Infantry, who, it turned out, was commanding the battalion in Fismes at that time; told him where we were, and asked him what he wanted us to do.

I learned from him that the situation was something like this: Part of the 112th Infantry were in a little town across the river called Fismette, where they were directly in touch with the enemy, fighting day and night. Fismes itself was for the most part ours. Germans were thought still to be in some of the houses sniping, or scattered along the railroad near the river. Most of the captain's battalion was scattered through Fismes in the cellars, and there was a part of the 109th Machine Gun Battalion near the town hall. During the day, a more or less stealthy man hunt went on from house to house, with occasional brisk fights, while the enemy shelled the town constantly from the heights across the river, throwing shells down into Fismes, sometimes in a barrage and sometimes intermittently. There was scarcely any time when you could not hear one bursting somewhere, followed by the slide and crumbling-sound of brick and plaster or the tinkle of glass. Having occupied the town for so long himself, "Fritz" was disgustingly familiar with it, and knew all the best places to shell.

The captain told me our best plan would be to find some more or less safe cellars, bring our men in, and leave them there for the night; after which he would move out when he could. The men over the river in Fismette would have to be relieved the next night, as it was too late to attempt it now, only a few hours before dawn.

Lieutenant Horner and I both left on the run and began to hunt for some convenient places. Up the street a house was burning, and as it flared up from time to time, I could see the tower of the town hall stand out, and the fronts of whole lines of empty houses up the street. Then the shadows would swoop down and engulf all.

I crossed the street and ran through what was evidently the gate of a big house. There was a large garden stretching several hundred yards down to the river in which a wrecked automobile was standing, and in the rear of the house I came across a dome-shaped structure made of large cut stones, cement, and railroad rails; this I knew was a dugout. Over the door was a board with a four-leaf clover on it and *"Villa Bremen"* in German letters. This I saw next day. A flight of carefully winding stone steps led down into the dark cement cavern, into which opened a wooden door. Holding up a lighted match, I discovered numerous old mattresses lying around and the dim outline of a door beyond that led into the depths of a large cellar, judging by the cold draft. Place number one—this would do! Running out, I met Horner hurrying up the street. He had found a big cellar vault under a seminary for his men, and was in luck.

There was no time to lose. No time to consider whether or not some enemy might not still be lurking about. Our men were out there by the bridge under fire, and every minute might mean lives. The next place I hit was a big club or hotel with a huge white, wooden gate that swung in. One look there was enough to assure me that there was room for an army, and best of all, a spigot was running in the court, gushing freely. That would be a godsend. Horner and I came out of our second places about the same time, and meeting up with the rest of the party, we raced down the littered street toward the bridge, where I was relieved to see that the barrage had lifted. So many stray shells were falling here and there that it was not till we got quite near that we could be sure of this.

Just on the other side of the bridge I met Captain Law. "I have a fine place, captain," I cried. "Thank God!" he said fervently, and the men near by scrambled to their feet expectant of the move. It must have been ticklish work lying there doing nothing. Horner ran back to his company. I sent a runner to inform the major, and we moved off in single file over the bridge, cautioning the men to be as silent as they could. As it was, the ring of the iron hobnails on the littered stone pavement seemed to make enough noise to alarm all the Germans between Fismes and Berlin.

I showed the captain the dugout I had found, and while he posted one platoon there, in the cellar, I went up the street with the others to put them to bed in the big club which, as I expected, had an ample cave-like vaulted cellar underneath. Sometimes I think the cellars of France did as much to win the war as the generals.

We certainly felt elated on having got the men into Fismes with so little loss. A few of the men were wounded by the barrage along the road, which, had it fallen a little to the left, would have landed on the highway with results appalling to think of. Such are the fortunes of war. A few feet one way or another is the difference between life and death. Getting such snug and safe places for the night, we also considered fortunate.

When I returned to the *"Villa Bremen,"* I found everybody preparing to turn in. One dim little candle was burning in the place, which was like a nice family tomb paved with mattresses. Beyond, in the dark cellar, the men could be heard stirring and clinking around from time to time, but most of them slept. It was very quiet down there. Even the sound of shells breaking in the street near by came only as dull thuds, shocks felt more than heard.

Toward the Flame

Our fortunate escape from the barrage, and the successful hunt for billets through the dark town, had so elated me that I remember boasting like a Turk about not seeing much to be afraid of in shell fire. I must really have made quite a cad of myself, as I remember some of the others, the poor captain particularly, who had had to lie still through all that rain of shells, looking at me rather disgustedly. My excitement and fatigue were beginning to tell. I actually plumped down on a mattress in the best corner, and when I accidentally put my feet on the captain, who had stretched out on the floor, I took his quiet remonstrance without feeling it. I had the best bed, too.

A few hours later, I woke up after a sound sleep

and, seeing him so uncomfortable on the floor, insisted on his coming over onto the mattress, with an excess of remorse for my callousness that nearly overcame me. He shook me by the hand. I shall never get over putting my feet on him that night. He was not to live very long.

Next morning it was quite late when I got up. Of course, no light penetrated the dugout, and in the cellar the worn-out men slumbered on night and day.

A little salmon and bread for breakfast—food was getting scarce—then I sallied out into the intense sunlight and the ruined town of Fismes.

It was nearly quiet at the time, only once in a while the long drone of a shell would pass overhead followed by a smash far off among the labyrinth of deserted houses. Now and then from over the river came the crack of a rifle. Crossing a street warily, I descended several flights of stone steps into a subcellar where I found Lieutenant Horner with his company. We decided to take a little walk about the town, and find out where we were.

Walking up the street, we were very wary and hugged the houses closely. The first place we dropped into was the clubhouse where I had billeted two of our platoons in the cellar the night before. Not a soul was to be seen when I pushed in the big, white gate that led into the court. The hydrant was still gushing away, but a hail brought some of the men out, blinking in the sunlight. They had been rummaging and showed us the house.

It had been the home of some club or society. Fismes was a large and rich town, and the "club" was luxuriously furnished. The Germans had been living here. Sofas and chairs sat around in vacant-looking groups. Tapestries and dirty, torn hangings flapped from the walls, where all the mirrors were cracked. The clocks and frescoes were defaced and names and vile pictures scribbled on the walls. Plaster dust was stamped all over the carpets that were covered with torn books and trash and ripped up in some places. The rear of the clubhouse opened onto a garden. Instead of a porch there was a partly demolished sun parlor with little iron tables and chairs like a French café. These sat around looking most forlorn. There were some empty bottles and glasses on them, dusty and full of flies. At the foot of the garden was a barn. Through the cracks in the rear door of it there was the vista of a path leading down through the interior of a partly demolished and abandoned steel mill. Beyond that lay the railroad, coal piles, and the sparkling river, then in flood. I established an observation post, and remembered that here was a short cut down this path to the river.

Across the street was a Roman Catholic seminary, a big building with wide, sweeping stairs and high ceilings. Here, too, had been a German billet. There was a hodgepodge of cast-off clothes and junk in the dormitories, where the Germans had slept in the rows of iron beds. We went up into the garret to get a view of the town. From the front windows we had a view of the handsome *Hôtel de Ville* with its clock tower, and the main square, very badly wrecked. The other windows showed us nothing but acres of slate roofs, with a cone-shaped hill in the distance. But the garret was quite interesting on account of its contents. Horner went down and left me alone for a while.

There was a poor little foot-organ that had been played to death, boxes of tinsel cards, plaster images of the saints, a portable altar, prayer books, school texts, vestments, a little English-French dictionary, which I took, and queer pious pictures. Some German soldier had come up there and changed his shoes, leaving the old worn-out boots with no toes standing side by side as mute witnesses of his visit. In one corner we found a small print shop with type already set, and the proof sheets of some strange little religious journal scattered about. How utterly futile it all seemed. The Virgin's heart, it seems, was yearning over the boys in the seminary who said their prayers to her. I added a footnote in penciled English about Mars. I wonder who read it:

> *"The Virgin is plucking asphodels in Heaven with little Saint John and the angels;*
> *Mars is walking the meadows of France, cutting the throats of God's sheep;*
> *The laughter of children has departed from this town. It is bereft forever."*

A German printer had come in and set something in German. The grinning, inked type stood fixed like tiny black teeth in the sheet which would never be finished. There were also piles and piles of wreaths of tinsel and paper flowers. Then I came downstairs and found some of our men stamping about. One platoon of "C" company was in the cellar.

While the place was so quiet, I felt determined to see the town, partly from curiosity and partly from a desire to know my way about the place in case of future necessity. I left Horner standing on the corner near the town hall, and made toward the cone-shaped hill I had seen from the garret windows of the seminary.

Imagine your own home town without a single soul in it, wrecked after a great storm, and partly burned, with all the evidences of the familiar activities of everyday life about, but that life and movement cut off suddenly, turned off like a light, and you will have a little idea of Fismes.

The looted stores stood gaping vacantly around the main square, where I met part of the machine gun battalion. They had their gun set up about halfway down a long hall that commanded a view of the street leading to the bridge. Rocks and earth were piled up as a sort of breastwork on the floor before it, and the ammunition was in the library. A corporal here warned me about the streets. One corner was bad for snipers. I could see it from the window upstairs and there was a dead runner lying there with the red band on his arm.

We dodged across the street to the town hall. This was a lovely white stone *Hôtel de Ville* with a mansard roof. There was a big wooden sign over the door in German, proclaiming it the Zone Kommandator's headquarters. The inside was badly wrecked. A mess of German and French town records lay all over the place. I found a chart

there showing a German plan of defense for Fismes and several maps of the town which I rolled up for our major. There were also several recent issues of German magazines.* *Die Woche,* and others. There was indeed a great deal of interesting German material. Among other things I picked up a post-card with the King of Saxony peering out between draped flags up in one corner, and below H. M., a rural scene with two little children hand in hand looking at a field full of cows. Underneath it said, "Little ones, do without milk so we can keep our colonies." How that must have appealed to the children!

I did not linger around the town hall very long as they were shelling that region pretty often, but headed back into some of the smaller streets, and edged over toward the hill, not so far off as I had thought.

Passing through the utterly empty streets was an eery experience. At one corner a German gunner lay dead by his machine gun. I think he had been hit by a big shell fragment, for his head was kicked in like a rotten pumpkin. He was short and thickset, a Bavarian, I think, with warts on his hands. Beside him was a gummy piece of bread made out of brown bran. Near by lay a number of empty cartridges, probably the last he had fired. The tremendously heavy boots and the iron helmet always lent the Ger-

* July, 1918, and a few months earlier.

mans a peculiarly brutal aspect. This man had turned the same dull gray as his coat, he had been dead so long. Poor devil, his interest in colonies had lapsed.

I felt pretty certain that that part of Fismes was no longer occupied by the enemy as it was too far back from the river, so I took a good many short cuts through the little lanes and finally, after crossing a spur of the railroad, I came out directly behind my little hill where there were several coal piles. The "Boche" had some curious shallow trenches dug on this elevation and there were several enormous shell craters near the top. This must at one time have been an observation station. I crawled when I got near the summit and, lying on my stomach, had an excellent view over the town. Its roofs stretched away from me to the bridge, beyond which lay the hillside and country on the other side of the Vesle. That was "Hunland" I was looking at over there.

A railroad ran along the river's edge, and there was a badly damaged stone bridge over the Vesle, with a hamlet on the far side stretching along a road paralleling the stream. Above all this rose the steep hillside occupied by the enemy, with draws here and there leading back to a sort of tableland behind, green with orchards and farms, but crossed now and then by a road. There was not a soul to be seen. Only now and then came a "boom," and a great geyser of mud and water shot up into the air beside the bridge.

I lay and examined the hill carefully and after

a while saw a man walking across a field. He came out of a clump of bushes, passed on down a path, moved over a field till he struck a road—up this he walked and disappeared. He was a German and looked like a pigmy over there on the great lone hill. That was all I saw of the enemy, although I watched for nearly an hour.

On the way back I noticed several very deep dugouts. The door of the house instead of opening into the hall had been made to open directly down a steep stairway that descended some thirty or forty feet. I think these had been built by the French inhabitants, as Fismes had been more or less under fire since the early days of the war. Alan Seeger speaks about that in his letters in 1914.

I found the major sheltered in the house right across the street from the *"Villa Bremen,"* and it was not long before a dressing station was established in the house above our dugout. The major looked over my town maps, but said he had a better one. By that time it was getting on toward noon, and the Germans began to shell the town violently, as they must have seen a lot of our men moving about the streets. The engineers had repaired the little bridge and an ambulance drove into the town and stopped before the door of the dressing station as if it were driving up to a house at home. Then two or three big shells went off in the house across the road and another fell directly into the street with a tremendous detonation. The major went into the cellar and I dodged across into the *"Villa Bremen."* I found that the Germans shelled our garden pretty often on account of the broken automobile there and because the ambulances could be seen coming up to "our door."

I found our cellar next to the dugout full of cases of potato-masher bombs and barrels of signal-lights which "Fritz" had left. These made us very uncomfortable. If a shell had come through the roof into that cellar, we would all have gone to glory in a burst of fireworks During the lulls the men therefore set these out in the garden, or shoved them into the street through the cellar windows. I went upstairs to take a shave while this was being done.

The house had evidently belonged to a well-to-do man, who had conducted some kind of an agricultural league or society, as near as I could make out. It was pitiable to see the desks and beautifully kept records and accounts all forced open and wasted around. In the office was a set of maps showing the growth of Paris from Roman times to the Third Empire. It was made from old prints and quaintly interesting. Private letters lay around in piles or strewn on the floor. To dip into these was always like tasting forbidden sweets or peeping in over a stranger's transom. "Before the war letters"—what a serene world that seemed now, to be sure: *"Cher Adolph: Le printemps est venu ici, nous"* . . . ridiculous!

Toward the Flame

I tried to shave at the kitchen sink; the water still ran in Fismes although somewhat feebly. There was the remains of the last meal the German orderly had prepared, yellow mayonnaise dressing and lettuce leaves in a pile of dirty plates. Outside was a glimpse of the old broken automobile in the yard, and the men carrying crates of bombs out of the cellar. Beyond was a vista down to the river bank.

I was only halfway through the shave when I heard a shell that I knew was coming very near. It burst in the yard and started the bombs going. There was a frightful series of explosions, during which I returned to the cellar, lather and all. Our dugout was proof against even a direct hit. I spent

most of the rest of the day in it, or in the cellar with the men. Food was already very scarce. The road into the town was being shelled so skillfully as to make it difficult for mess details to get in or out. We sent one detail, but it was impossible to spare a good leader at the time, so it came back. I could not spare the sergeants for mess details. The 112th had left that morning, all but the men across the river in Fismette, whom we found it impossible to relieve that day.

Into the Pit

Intense firing could be heard over there from time to time.

The rumor here was that when we drove the enemy over the hill on the other side of the Vesle, we were to go back for a rest. "The general had said so"— as usual just what general was not specified. At any rate we were to make an attack, and the captain was going with the major next morning to make a reconnaissance. We went to sleep early with very little supper. It seemed already as if we had been in Fismes a great many days.

CHAPTER XV

A WILD DAY

AFTER the *strafing* of the day before, the major moved his headquarters to the cave where I had first found the captain of the 112th on the night we entered Fismes. I found a short cut to it from our own hole in the ground through several connecting gardens and down a little pair of steps. In the largest of these gardens there were one or two graves of men of the 110th U. S. Infantry. The short cut kept us off the streets away from snipers and shells.

A Wild Day

That morning the major and the captain, with some of the other company commanders, left on the reconnaissance, going down the river to an old tannery a mile or so away. A lot of the men were ordered out on detail to carry wounded back from Fismette. This left me, with the mess details that were already out, about thirty men altogether. Some were billeted in the *"Villa Bremen,"* and some in the cellar at the "club." There was a great deal of firing all morning over in Fismette, and enemy planes came over Fismes several times, after which a bombardment more or less intense would follow.

The German artillery back among the hills must have had a good time shelling their old homes. Our house was gunned for persistently on account of the dressing station being there, and about one o'clock they made a direct hit on the dugout. Several of us were sitting around smoking on the mattresses, when there was a noise and a skull-cracking jar that almost stunned us. It was hard to think for a minute or so afterwards. Our ears were so numbed that everything seemed very silent for some time. Everybody cowered down; there was the trickle of dirt on us from the ceiling, and dust in the air. But the tremendously thick stone, cement, and iron rails still held. Only a few of the outer layers were dislodged although it was a 6-inch shell.

We kept pretty "close" after that for some time. I opened a precious tin of beef, and we were just

going to eat it when some one opened the door and
called down. It was very silent in the dugout, but
as soon as any one opened the door there came down
the stairs a tremendous din of firing, machine guns
chattering, the crack of rifles, and the smash of shells
booming among the houses. It was the major at
the door.

"The Germans are making a counter attack!" cried
he, "get the men out, and in line!" I left the top
sergeant tumbling the men out of our cellar, while I
ran up the street to the "club," where part of another
platoon was billeted. Both the major and the adjutant kept begging me, almost beseeching me, to
hurry. I supposed, of course, that the Germans had
penetrated the town again.

A very few moments sufficed to get the men together at the "club." The sergeants exerted themselves to the utmost, hauling men out of the dark
cellars and getting the equipment on them like har-
nessing fire horses. As soon as we were sure we
had the cellar clear, we started on a run for the
"Villa Bremen," where I found the rest of the men
waiting in the garden. These were tag ends of all
the platoons, as the mess details, the men detailed
to carry wounded, and those detached to battalion
headquarters had left us with a very small remnant
of our three-platoon company, already small to begin
with.

A Wild Day

With what non-coms I had, we formed the men rapidly into squads and made on a run for the lower part of the garden. There we crawled through a fence and went into skirmish line, deploying in a field that led straight down to the river and the railroad track. On our right was the old steel mill and the rear of the houses that faced on the street going down to the bridge. On our left, near the river, was a big factory of some kind. I took all this in at a glance. The excitement photographed it forever on my retina. Danger makes one live intensely.

It was our intention to take up a position along the river, using the railway embankment as a trench to resist the enemy should they attempt to cross the stream. I instructed the first sergeant, who had about half the men, to move over into the factory on the left as we advanced. After taking a few seconds to get the automatic rifle teams * and the skirmish line properly disposed, we started forward on the double.

The sergeant led his men off to the left, while we made straight for the river, a stretch of about two hundred yards. About halfway the enemy turned his machine guns on us. The air suddenly seemed to be alive with a swarm of vicious wasps and I saw the dust cut up all about our feet. There were one or two cries, but we were moving too fast to find out who it was that had been hit. I thought the fire was

* These men were armed with the French *Chauchat* automatic rifle.

coming from behind a huge coal pile directly in front of us and led the way straight for it. We were all greatly bewildered and the men bunched. There was a dreadful second or two when I could not get them started toward the pile. Then Sergeant Griffin jumped out and started with me, and the rest closed in with their bayonets. We came onto the pile with a fierce rush. There was nothing there!

I got the platoon sheltered behind it and looked about me. About fifty yards back were three or four quiet bundles that had been men a few seconds before. I watched them from time to time, but there was no more movement. They were dead, not wounded. That coal pile was about thirty feet high, made of brickets and slack which stopped shells excellently. It stretched along the railroad track for some seventy-five feet or so. Just behind us was a very deep hole, a little railroad switchman's house, the upper part of which was was glass, and a long, low dugout, like an Eskimo's igloo, that was capable of sheltering twenty or thirty men.

The air was still full of the vicious *ttt-ang* of bullets over our heads, and, of course, the Germans had seen us take shelter behind the coal. The machine gun fire which had caught us came from guns across the river, high up on the hillside almost a mile away. There was no attack on at all. Everything was quieting down, but we were in such a position that we would have to wait till dark to get back to the town.

226

A Wild Day

To move back in any numbers meant to be shot up again.

I sent a runner back to the captain with a sketch of our position and got one of the men to crawl over to Sergeant Davidson in the factory telling him where we were and our plans. About an hour later the runner to the captain returned, having crept through the steel mill and along the railroad track. The enemy sniped at us continually. To put one's helmet over the top of the pile was to draw bullets instantly. We saw some of our men attacking a house on the other side of the river. Several of them were brought down and Sergeant Griffin located a German sniper who was standing back in a room out of our fellows' line of sight calmly firing at them. Griffin took a rifle and after long and careful aim from the side of the coal pile brought the German down. He hung down out of the window. Our men on the other side instantly closed in on the house which was near the bridgehead in Fismette.

Our own position was absurd. The river in front of us was too deep to be crossed in

force, and the little footbridge was nearly wrecked. There was no counter attack. If there ever had been any, it was across the river in Fismette, and it had now subsided. We were simply caught in the open space between the town and the river and had to wait till dark, keeping behind the coal pile. In the meantime I shifted all the men I could move back into the dugout on the other side of the ditch, and put the rest of the men in the ditch where I crawled myself. This was simply a rather deep cut worn by the rainwater where it had run down to a little drainage culvert under the tracks. It was well we moved there.

All the activity the Germans had seen on our side of the river, crossing the fields in skirmish order, etc., had alarmed them. I think they must have thought an attack was preparing on *our* part, for just about twilight they poured a barrage along the river front and into the town. In the waning light we sat huddled in the ditch while the wailing shells came over.

An experience of that kind can never be described. Death is very near. There is a constant howling shuddering the air, and shells were dropping everywhere about us. I expected a direct hit every minute, but the coal pile saved us. It mercifully cut off the shells just in the angle of their drop. Then some shrapnel came over. One of our men, a big Montenegrin, who had been wounded by a machine gun bullet in the arm during the futile rush on the coal pile, was hit by shrapnel fragments in the other arm, while several of the men got other wounds in various places. Slivers and rocks rattled off our tin hats constantly. Finally one lad, who had crawled halfway into the drain partly to shelter his body, got a sickening shrapnel cut in the leg. We had a hard time to stop the hemorrhage, the blood spurted all over us; naturally enough, he was terrorized. Jack, the Montenegrin, was as brave as he could be and sat with set jaw. He must have been in extreme pain.

The roar of the explosions about us was almost continuous. The air was full of peculiar black smoke, dust, débris, and the stifling odor of high explosive, luckily no gas. During one of the short lulls we saw some of our men running along the railroad track

like figures in a fog. These were some of the lads
the first sergeant had led to the factory. They had
been shelled out of that, and came scudding through
the haze and dust like birds in a storm, plunging
down into our little ditch and filling it to the point of
crowding. I had to take stern measures here to make
place for all. Some of them we shouted to, or they
would never have seen us. I shall never forget how
weird and weak our voices sounded in that great
uproar. One or two of those who had been in the
factory were wounded too. They lay quiet and
shook through the rest of the barrage which followed. About dark it let up with an occasional shell
howling now and then, but these finally died away,

230

leaving a heavy silence. I waited till I was sure that it was over and then sent the men back by twos and threes, getting the wounded out first. Through the darkness, shaking and quivering, we sneaked back to the ghostly, white town.

The men who had been killed had had their lives wasted after a certain manner. Boys playing Indian would have known enough to stick to the houses if there *had been* an attack. But there is an aphorism about the reticence of dead men who are the only competent witnesses to this kind of fooling.

CHAPTER XVI

OVER THE BRIDGE

ONE can well imagine that after the experience of the afternoon we were pretty well fagged out mentally and physically, so that when the captain told me we were to cross the bridge that night into Fismette, relieve the 112th there, and make an attack, I was not exactly enthusiastic.

Nothing was said to the men. There is no use worrying soldiers in advance. Somehow, I could not fully realize that after the miracle of coming through unharmed that afternoon, the whole process would have to be repeated. One always felt subconsciously, "Surely, surely, this is enough!" Then we were tired, very tired, so I lay down on one of the mattresses and slept—more than slept—I died for a few hours.

About two o'clock I wakened to find the captain shaking me in the dim yellow light of one candle burning without a flicker in the calm and silence of the dugout. The feeling that we were going into battle was so distasteful and so strong that it was like mental indigestion. One felt weak, and I realized that the only thing to do was to get moving and doing something quickly. The captain was telling me the plans.

We were to cross the bridge into Fismette, march down the river about a mile to an old Tannery, where we were to join hands with our second battalion, and then move up the hill in attack.

"Get the men ready," said the captain. "Issue extra ammunition and bombs."

There was no ration to issue. Our mess detail had failed to get through to the ration dump that afternoon for the second time. We knew that there was still some of the emergency, or "iron ration," as it was called, left among the men, although many must have eaten much of this during the hungry time of the last three or four days.

The emergency ration consisted of two or three

little red cans full of corned beef, known as "monkey meat," and hard crackers in long pasteboard boxes, the hard bread, or "hard-tack," of fame. Sometimes we got the French hard bread that was like a round rusk and was issued loose. All this the men were not supposed to eat without a direct order, but under actual conditions, with the companies scattered about in cellars, very hungry, and in no fear of inspections, it was almost impossible to prevent nibbling. One can scarcely court-martial a man on the firing line for eating a cracker after having gone without food for many hours. It takes a professional martinet to punish a man for that.

I went into the adjoining cellar and wakened the top sergeant, who in a few minutes had the men stirring. They were to come up the street to the "club" and rendezvous with the rest of the platoons there. I learned that the captain would really be in charge of the battalion, as the major did not intend to accompany us in the attack. He was to remain in his command post in Fismes.

As I ran up the street to the club, I could hear the din of the firing in Fismette, and see the white glare made by the German flares. Getting the men out of the huge, dark cellar was not easy. They were all worn out and kept dropping off to sleep again. At last we got them lined up in the court and started to issue ammunition and grenades. The excitement now swept me along so I was going strong. Getting the grenades open was difficult as they were in wooden boxes tightly screwed down. We split these with our bayonets and found inside the deadly pear-shaped objects. These were French *citron grenades* with a tin cylinder at one end which you pulled off, exposing a spring and plunger. The plunger, when struck on your helmet or any convenient object, set off the grenade, the explosion following five or six seconds later. The men had been taught in grenade school, but I made sure they all knew how to operate these.

Then we took our precious rockets, now much the worse for wear, looking like a leftover from last Fourth of July. I begged the ammunition officer for some rifle grenades, but none were issued. Most of the men had thrown away their *tromblones** anyway. I found this often happened in other commands. In the darkness the court seemed to swarm with the men. As they filed out the gate the seeming confusion died down and each man received his grenade. That seemed to sober them. It looked like business. At the last, two or three stragglers ran up the steps from the cellar followed by the sergeants, who had done their best to turn everybody out. Despite this, a few remained, some asleep, and some slackers, well-hidden in the long vaulted cellar. There was no time to hunt through this. Some men of the machine gun

* Funnel-shaped caps fitted on the end of a rifle from which the grenade was thrown by shooting the gun.

battalions were also sleeping down there. Our little three-platoon company was down to one hundred and twenty men that night. We led the column.

I found the captain waiting in the street until the platoons came out of the gate. He was impatient at the time we had taken to fall in, which doubtless seemed long to him waiting there in suspense. We moved off down the street in single file, hugging the side of the houses to avoid being seen when the flares went up. I could hear the shuffle and crackle of the men's feet among the loose slate and débris, while the long caterpillar of "the relief" wound around the corner at the city hall and started down toward the bridge. As we got near the bridge, where flares went up from time to time, the whole stealthy line would stop, lost in the waning, flickering, monstrous shadows cast by the Véry lights that floated in a string of little parachutes for a few seconds and then drifted to earth, to quench themselves in a sea of ink. Then darkness shut down like a lid. There were no orders needed when to halt; the men did it by instinct, the old instinct that keeps the rabbit still even when the hound comes sniffing near. The Germans were very close.

There was a halt for a minute or two at the bridge before we left the shelter of the last house. This, in order to see that the column was well "closed up." Then we started over, making a tremendous noise it seemed.

At the end of the town there was the flash and crackle of rifle fire. The Germans had been bursting shells on the bridge for several days and the stone above the arch had in one place been blown through, making an oval dip about the middle of the bridge with half of the roadway blown away, showing the river underneath. Big stones from the coping lay scattered about on the top of the bridge itself, and in one place only was there a section about two feet wide on which to cross. The river below was a tangle of débris, a snarl of old wire. The mud banks were splashed and pitted with shell-holes where the mud geysers had spouted over everything when the shells lit. Over this bridge we started, hoping fervently the enemy machine gunners would not see us. About fifty yards up the road, on the other side, some of our men in a ruin were fighting the Germans across the street in another house. The firing through windows and from between cracks in the walls lit the night fitfully.

The captain crossed first, and turned to the left on the other side followed by the men in file. We went through a gutted house and out into the village street beyond. I stood at the bridge, keeping the men closed up until our last platoon was over, and I saw "A" company following. As the captain turned to the left, I heard two or three rifle cracks but paid no attention to them at the time. As soon as the company was over I hastened to catch up with him again.

But when I turned the corner into the single lonely street of Fismette, I found three or four of our lads gathered about the body of one of our own men. It was Charley Wright, from whose helmet the spent bullet had glanced when we came into Fismes. He had been shot by one of our own men, having for some reason or other stepped out into the street between the houses where the fighting had been going on. He was certainly dead. It seemed tremendously futile.

I ran on down the street past our own men, now halted and hugging the houses closely, till I came to the head of the column. The captain was standing shouting at an officer of the 112th. The din ahead was tremendous. About a square away a trench mortar shell was falling every fifteen seconds.

We were, as you may remember, supposed to move

on down the river a mile and join hands with the second battalion at the Tannery, to make an attack. The orders, of course, had been written by some one looking at a map, and typed in a comfortable billet some twenty or thirty kilometers in the rear.

I heard the lieutenant of the 112th roar, "Mile! nothing! You can only go another block. We have only half the town; 'Fritz' owns the rest. The Prussian Guard is right across the street." His remarks were punctuated by the rocking explosions of the trench mortar shells. In the gray light I looked about me.

We were in a straight village street packed solid with houses on either side. The back doors of one line of houses opened out onto a field that stretched on a gentle slope about two hundred yards down to the river. From the back yards of the buildings on the other side of the street rose a steep hill. The Germans were up there somewhere. Ahead was a cross street where there was the almost constant flash of mortar shells. A whole battery was playing on it from the heights above. There was only one thing to do, occupy all the town that we could, and hold it. The 112th man was too impatient to leave to give us much information. I didn't blame him. I wished he were relieving us.

The captain and I went with him along the street for another block, and at the end of this, a little way back from the street crossing, was a low half

breastwork, half barricade of barrels, furniture, and big stones across the street. Several of the 112th were lying behind this, firing up the street. I caught a glimpse of some skulking gray figures up there in the doorways. We turned aside into a house, went upstairs and looked out of the rear windows.

It was very early dawn, almost dark yet, and in the dust drifting back from the shell bursts we could see very little. Right below our window there was the beginning of a thin line of our men that stretched at right angles to the village street almost down to the river. Some were in shell-holes, and others in little pits that they had dug. In the obscurity there was only the dim outline of the prone figures, but from them, and beyond into the darkness, sprang out the stabbing jets from the rifles and the flash, flash, flash from the automatics.

We could see nothing of the Germans, but by now there was the constant shuddering of shells passing overhead and the crash where they burst in great columns of water and mud down at the bridge. The red flash of one would light up the spurts of those already exploding. By this time, though, our men were all over the bridge. We stood there only a few seconds watching, awed by the tremendousness of the spectacle, but, I remember, quite calm. That it was impossible to push on to the Tannery was too evident to be even discussed.

"What do you think we had better do?" I asked the captain. I was thinking of an attack by the Germans from the rear hillside and pointed this possibility out to him.

He ordered me to lead the first two platoons up the hill, back of the houses on the other side of the street, and take the best position I could find. I was also to relieve the men of the 112th that we saw from the window with our third platoon, all that we had in Company "B." This meant simply that at the barricade two platoons turned to the right up the hill on one side of the street, and one platoon to the left down toward the river. The captain himself went back to instruct the other company commanders of the change in plans.

I lost no time, but dodged across the street and

through one of the half-ruined houses on the other side. There was a long hall, but the back door opened on a garden with high walls and a barn between it and the cross street, so we were hidden. The garden was very steep, going up the hill about fifty yards to a wall with some scraggly trees along it that seemed to extend along all the back yards of the village, parallel with the street. To jump back into the street and beckon the men toward me was the work of a few seconds only.

Glendenning led the way, a tower of strength in time of need as usual. I scarcely had to say anything to him. He took in the plan of taking up position behind the wall at a glance. I had to stay in the doorway to turn the third platoon the opposite way when it came up. It was in charge of a young lieutenant of the 77th Division who had just joined us. I forget his name. He was a little chap, but one of the bravest, gamest, little fellows that ever lived, and he handled his men like a veteran. I told him what his position was to be and saw some of our men lie down beside the 112th at the barricade across the street. Just then the captain joined me. As we went down the long hall to the garden, I saw a picture on the wall by the flash of a shell that lit in the garden ahead. A lot of plaster fell behind us.

We ran up the garden as fast as we could, for the shell had knocked part of a barn down. The ascent was very steep at the back. The last of the men were just scrambling up this when another shell lit in the barn again right behind us. After that they continued to fall there for some time.

It was a very near thing. The Germans must have seen us passing there. They evidently had wonderful *liaison* with their trench mortars to switch the fire so quickly. The captain went right up to the wall and told me to work down to the right and see if we were connecting with "C" company there. It was the last time I ever saw him.

The wall was only about knee-high in places, sometimes only a few stones for quite a stretch. Behind this our men lay firing at nothing. From somewhere was coming a perfect hail of machine gun bullets, mostly over our heads, but the worst of it was that some of it was coming from the flanks. We were beautifully enfiladed, probably by some guns away up on the hills above us a mile away. In the darkness this could not have been foreseen. It was plain right away that to keep the men in line along that wall was suicidal, but, of course, I could do nothing as I was not in command. I tried to stop the men from firing at nothing as I went along, but control was out of the question. One had to hug the ground close, backing down the slope a little in order to crawl toward the right. In a little hollow I came across a group. Lieutenant Glendenning and one or two sergeants were stooping over Lieutenant Larned, another of the 77th officers. He had been shot in the throat and was choking in his own blood. He lay quiet but was still alive. There was nothing we could do. I spoke to him, but he shook his head. Then I told Glendenning where I was going, and crawled on. It was the last time I ever saw *him* alive.

When I finally reached the left flank of our company line I found the wall had gaps in it here and there. Through these the machine gun barrage poured, striking the roofs of the houses at the bottom of the garden. The slate slithered off like scales. Behind one clump of rocks and stones was a squad of our men firing at a haystack, while in a sort of hollow of the hill, and just rising above its crest, was the roof mass of another hamlet. I felt sure some of the fire must be coming from there. The men said there was a machine gun in the haystack. Away to the left was a half-burnt house. There was barbed wire about it. The rest was just orchards and fields. Not a sign of any living thing. Out of this apparent void was coming the deadly hail that was killing us. Here and there along the wall I saw men tearing open their first-aid packages. That something must be done was evident. A change of position would have to be made, or there would be no one to change.

Just then I saw the men getting up from the left all along the line, waver a minute and then move forward.

I motioned forward to the line ahead of me and

244

jumped up with them leading out into the fields up
the hill. The machine guns were like a hundred riv-
eters going all at once, such a chattering I never
heard. Just where we were there was a little draw
in the hill which seems to have saved us. At that
part of the line we advanced about fifty yards, I
judged. Looking back, I saw the rest of the line returning. There was absolutely no place to advance
to. It was a brave but senseless attack. Some of the
men lay down and fired where they were. I think I
took about six men back with me behind the wall in
my section of the line. Most of those who lay out in
the fields were killed, but a few crawled back that
night. The captain was killed in this attack, but I

245

did not know that until hours later. He had ordered it.

It was so evident that another position would have to be taken up quickly that I determined to find Lieutenant Horner of "C" company and make arrangements with him, captain or no captain. It was no longer a question of waiting for orders but of holding the town. Accordingly, I told one of the sergeants of "C" company where I was going, and gave him strict orders to hold until he got word to move. I then crawled down a path between the houses to the street. If it was bad by the wall, it was worse in the street. A stream of machine gun bullets was racing past. It sounded like sawing. I crawled along close to the houses where Lieutenant Glendenning was afterwards killed, and got across the street by a rain ditch. By this time crawling like a turtle seemed to be the most natural form of movement in the world. Any other method I could not even think of. I met Horner with one runner moving along in the rear of the houses evidently trying to pick a new and more sheltered position. We held a very hasty but very serious consultation.

Comparing notes, it was perfectly evident that there could no longer be any question of attack, and that if we did not receive reënforcements *and ammunition* and get the help of a barrage on the hillside to clean the enemy out, we should not long be able to hold the town. Both of us felt that a message could not explain the situation which had already been so utterly misunderstood on the other side of the river. If an officer could get across, it might be made clear and the coördinates could be given for the barrage. It would not do to trust that to an enlisted man. Horner could not swim, so it was up to me.

I left a message for the captain, telling him what I was going to try to do. Horner shook hands, wished me good luck, and I started.

CHAPTER XVII

OVER THE RIVER AGAIN

IT had been my intention at first to cross by the bridge, but one look at the barrage falling there marked it off the slate of possibilities. There was a barrage all along the river front, but especially heavy at the bridge. The shells arriving there and along the stream were very large ones, throwing up immense fountains of liquid mud and exploding in the water with a peculiar muffled crack and roar. As I watched them I nearly turned back; it seemed such a futile task. Only a fool would have dashed out.

A little study showed that away from the bridge there were considerable intervals of time between shells, and that they were pretty well scattered. I also noted a small drainage ditch across the field running down to the river. Along this was the path which led to the ruined wooden footbridge, now floating level with the water and partly shot away. I could see the tangle of it from Fismette. Through the barrage haze Fismes looked miles away, the white houses standing out more plainly in the sun.

The ditch was the only thing that could enable one to reach the river. My body lay in the hollow, so the machine gun barrage went over me. . . .

It took me about half an hour to crawl to the river. I had to put my mask on at the last, as the mustard gas was strong in the little hollow in which I lay. My hands were smarting. Some of the shells brought my heart into my mouth; lying there waiting for them was intolerable. I was sure I was going to be blown to pieces. The river was very nearly in flood and so there was no bank, the field gradually getting soggy and swampy till it sloped out into the water. There was a lot of submerged barbed wire that made going ahead very painful and slow. I had, of course, to throw away my mask as it got full of water. My pistol went also. It was too heavy to risk.

Once in the water, I worked under the single board of the footbridge, shifting along hand over hand, which took me halfway across. There I struck out, plunging in a few strokes to the other side and working through the wire.* Swimming with shoes was not so difficult as I had thought, but the cold water seemed to take all my courage, which was what I needed more than ever. Our own machine guns were playing along the railroad track on our side of the river. After getting across, it seemed for a while that I would be caught between the two fires.

I lay there in the river for a minute and gave up. When you do that something dies inside.

Then I saw the culvert under the track leading into the hole where we had lain during the barrage of the night before. I crawled through this and into the dugout at its edge, taking great care not to show myself for fear some of our own snipers might pick me up.

The luxury of that place was immense. I was safe there, safe, for a few minutes! I forgot everything but my own escape. The river had washed most of the mustard gas off, too. Only my eyes still smarted. A very few minutes, however, brought on a nausea that made me afraid I should not be able to cover the rest of my trip. I crawled out of the dugout very warily, still afraid of our own machine guns and the guns across the river that had picked us up the day

* It should be remembered that the Vesle is not a "river" in the American sense of the word; it is really a "creek" across which one could shy a stone.

before, and finally made way through the ruined steel mill which kept me out of sight most of the distance. It had a long shed. Then I took the little path straight up to the barn behind the "club" which we had occupied, and shoving the door aside, stepped into the courtyard and sat down.

Some of the machine gun men there jumped up rather startled, and then came over to give me a lift, but I was able to go on all right after a few minutes' breathing, and made my own way to the major's dugout.

They must have been shelling Fismes very heavily that morning, for the little lane leading to the wine cave was literally strewn with dead runners. The air

was heavy with gas, the effect of which I could now plainly feel, a sort of tightening across the lungs and a burning rawness. Not having a mask worried me greatly. There was an old blanket over the door to keep out the gas, and as I went in I noticed a big unexploded air bomb just on the bank above. How it got there I do not know. I lifted the blanket and stepped inside.

The major was telephoning to the colonel as I came in, using the line which the signal corps had established with great difficulty. The different telephones had queer names in order to give no information in case the enemy listened in. I remember the major was talking to "Hindu" something. He was telling the colonel that the attack was so far going well and that we were taking prisoners. I believe some Germans had been taken somewhere, which gave him the impression that we were having a great success. It did not take me very long to give him the real situation, and a very different story went over the wire than had been started. The gravity of affairs was at once apparent.

That dugout was absolutely packed. All the battalion scouts, the runners from all the different organizations in *liaison* with us,* a good many wounded, and some simply taking shelter filled the place to the stifling point. In addition there were a good many officers—the captain of our machine

* Runners were interchanged.

gun company, which had just moved into Fismes,
our battalion scout officer, and several others from
the third battalion that was just then entering the
town. Runners were coming and going.

The major and his adjutant sat at a table with
a map on which we were soon drawing the lines for
the barrage with an artillery *liaison* officer super-
intending the job. We drew them in a horseshoe
curve well above the town to avoid the possibility
of "shorts" among our own men. Pretty soon the
artillery lieutenant was telephoning to the batteries,
but the line was cut about this time and there was
a maddening delay. I asked for a gas mask and

one was taken from a dead man near the door. There were no extras about.

Things began to get pretty hazy for me about this time. I remember giving a book of notes and poems to our scout officer. It was soaked with water but not ruined. Some of the men helped me out of my pack. The river water I had swallowed was the last touch.

Major Donnely, the commanding officer of the third battalion, came in now. He grew very angry at the crowded condition of the dugout and made some of the men move out to other shelter, ordering them to keep away from the door where they cut off what little air there was. Shells were falling outside every few minutes. Between them Godfrey Wyke skipped in, neat, lively, and the same as ever. He and the other company commanders of the third battalion were called in for a little council, and it was decided that after dark an attempt would be made to reënforce the first battalion in Fismette. About this time a runner came in from the other side of the river. He had gotten across the bridge in a lull. The intensity of the barrage after our attack had now relaxed greatly. The message told us that Captain Law of my company had been killed, that the captain of "A" company was wounded, and that the men had been safely withdrawn to the town, but needed reënforcements and ammunition. I said I would guide the reënforcing companies back that night. There was some good news, though. A platoon of the 109th machine gun battalion had crossed the river higher up and worked into Fismette.

After an hour or two the nausea passed off, and the major gave me some cornbeef hash, but I was not quite able to get away with it. After sitting around an hour, I got up and went out with our ammunition officer to see if we could get down to the river and "ferry" some boxes across, near to the little footbridge.

We moved very carefully, cutting across the road just behind an ambulance that drove by at reckless speed. Another was loading just across the street from the house above the *"Villa Bremen."* The lieutenant and I went up to the "club" and took a peep at the river from the barn. The whole bank was still being torn up by the shells, a lot of which were also falling in the fields and through the town.

As soon as I saw that hell-hole, I knew absolutely that I didn't have the courage to try it again. Whether we ever could have carried ammunition boxes through that gantlet and then floated them across the river on planks I do not know. But I do know I didn't have the courage then to head the gang that was going to try it. The ammunition officer said nothing one way or the other. I was so tired I didn't care what he thought. While we stood there looking, our own barrage fell around Fismette.

Imagine that little white town up on the hillside, and just above and around it in a semi-horseshoe a great waving cloud of black dust, spurting earth fountains, smoke and flying dirt as though giants were throwing wagonloads of it into the air. There was a howling and whistling overhead and a steady roar from the other side of the river. This kept up for about a half hour, after which there was a dead silence for a long time. I hated to tell the major that I couldn't get the ammunition across, so I went over to the *"Villa Bremen"* and slept. The quiet, the coolness, the sense of isolation in the dugout was grateful. One of the medical men was there. Now and then we could hear the dull thud of a shell. It seemed far away. "Doc" got me a little cornbeef hash. I slept till four o'clock, it being impossible to stay awake any longer.

When I woke I seemed to have slept off most of the dizzy feeling of the morning. I had pretty well breathed myself clear of the sick gas feeling and was able to think clearly again. I went over to the major's dugout and found two engineer officers there with the two majors. We talked over the possibility of rebuilding the little footbridge across the river. I thought that it might be possible to slip down at night and reconstruct this bridge out of the material lying around near by, light trusses from the near by steel mill and heavy fence planks. It was a very short span. Things had quieted down now, and I took the two engineer officers, a major and a captain to look at the footbridge. We tried to get as near as possible without being seen.

The landscape about Fismes and Fismette that mellow summer afternoon about the middle of August is indelibly printed on my memory. We went down through the "club" again. A shell had broken all the glass out of the little sun parlor. It lay about in great sword-like splinters sparkling and twinkling on the iron wine tables and chairs. Then we cut out through the barn and down the path through the steel mill towards the railroad. Here I could point out the wreck of the little plank suspension bridge floating on the turbid, muddy current rolling by so rapidly. Across there was the little town of Fismette, just then so quiet, so white on the green vacant hillside, and the ruined buildings and back lots of Fismes with the railroad stretching along the river. Almost any moment one could expect a train to come puffing around the curve. It seemed so peaceful. But there was a caution, a fear that kept us from showing ourselves, that made us glide quietly, quickly by open spaces between buildings, an expectancy, a breathlessness, an unnatural calm that meant war.

We went back to the command post. The engineers were to try that night to build the bridge, but we could not wait for that, and it was decided to attempt the reënforcement of Fismette by sending over "L" and "M" companies of the third battalion, with part of "I" company equipped with stretchers, to bring out the wounded as soon as it was thoroughly dark. We were going to try to cross by the ruined stone bridge, hoping we could sneak in. I was to guide them, since I had been over once and knew the ropes.

Supper was very intense that night. Ten or twelve men of our own battalion who had remained behind the night before, for one reason or another, were to go over with us also, and they were not very cheerful. The ration was very scarce. Some salmon and half-raw canned sweet potatoes. I took leave of *"Villa Bremen"* again with regret, and went across the street to find Captain Keel of "L" company with his outfit. He was lining them up in the courtyard of the seminary ready to march. In the fast-failing light they looked tremendously grim and business-like. "L" company was about the finest body of men I ever saw. A few houses up the street "M" company was waiting under Captain Thompson, a fiery, determined little soldier; to talk to him for a few minutes in the street gave one renewed nerve. He had an intrepid personality. With him in charge, we were halfway over already.

He gave the word and the two companies came filing out of the houses in single file, just as we had moved the night before.

Over the River Again

We started to make stealthily for the bridge. The men had all been warned, and this time moved with great care. As we got near the river the flares began to stop us. Again and again came the green-white light, and again and again we froze into silence and stillness. One saw the skeleton houses, windows agape, the rows on rows of slate roofs, the tense, silent line of white faces under the helmets—swoop came the shadows, blackness and night—then we moved on again.

About a block from the bridge one of the platoon on guard there came back to tell us that the German machine guns played on it whenever the slightest noise was made by any one crossing. He told us an encouraging tale of several runners who had been killed that afternoon trying to get across. The story completely sickened me. I lost for a moment all the resolution I had. "No more machine guns, no more!" I kept saying to myself against my will. Just then a flare went up, and we halted. I told the news to Captain Thompson, who kept the men halted and ordered them to sit down. Captain Keel came up and suggested sending a message back to the major to apprise him of the situation. This gave some excuse to ourselves for a delay. At least we needed a little time to con the affair over. To be stopped at the bridge would be to bring down a barrage that would make the reënforcement of Fismette impossible. Captain Thompson wanted to get some information from the machine gun outfit who had been near the bridge all day. So one of the machine gun company stationed near here led us into a big house. The outer doors were closed fast after we entered. Then we went through a hall and another door was closed. After this a light was lit and we descended into a big cellar. The whole machine gun company seemed to be there, and very comfortable. Lieutenant Dan Brooks, a light-hearted, generous youth, was in charge. We drank some white wine, of which there were several barrels about. It was the last time I ever saw Dan Brooks. He laughed, gave us some information, wished us good luck, and shook hands. Thompson and I looked at each other—there was no excuse for any further delay. Now was as good as any other time.

We left Brooks in the cheerful candlelight and sallied out through the big door of the house and down the steps to our men sitting silently along the sides of the houses as we had left them. Thompson gave the word, and in a moment we were under way again, making rapidly but carefully for the bridge. At the bridge we halted sheltering behind the last houses.

Keel, who was leading "L" company, and I went first. I remembered passing two of our snipers at the bridgehead, lying behind a stone with their rifles ready. They were going to fire at the flash if a gun spoke. One of them whispered to me, "Don't stoop down, lieutenant, they are shooting low when they cut loose." Then we went out onto the bridge.

It was much more damaged than the night before, big stones blown loose all over it, holes in the middle, the pit of the night before much enlarged. As we descended into this a flare went up. That was undoubtedly the most intense moment I ever knew. For me, it was the great moment of the war. I was sure we must be seen. We stood rigid. The flare rose, drifted to the ground, and went out—not a shot! The last half we made in a silent but brief scramble.

There was not a soul on the other side, but I am afraid to say how many dead lay around the house at the head of the bridge. I threw a stone back, which was the signal agreed upon, and the men began to come over, three at a time and very quietly, crouching so that they looked like the big stones when a flare went up. After about twenty were over I started into the town by the back way, leading the file through several houses and twists and turns to a barricade across the street. At every corner a man was left to keep saying, "This way, this way." It was essential not to lose contact here. The line kept feeding across without a hitch, man after man crouching down to cross the village street behind the barrels filled with stone that led over into the doorway of a big barn. It was a combination barn and house around a big central court. At the upper end of it was a wine cave that went into the almost perpendicular hill.

Out of this came Captain Haller, who was in charge of what was left of the first battalion in Fismette. He was rather startled at first at seeing so many silent figures in the courtyard, but his welcome was more than hearty. In a few minutes the new men were being stationed. Some were sent up on the line to relieve the tired watchers there, others to sleep in lofts, a cellar or a house, but all ready for instant call. We brought in with us several

bags of ammunition, grenades, and litters to carry out the wounded, whose evacuation was started immediately.

It was half an hour before the Germans "got wise" and started to gun for the bridge. In the meantime the town had been reënforced.

"Fritz" was very near here. From a little hamlet, the cluster of roofs just up the hill back of our barn and cave, he shot flares right down into the court. Captain Haller came out and put up a red rocket. I remember him standing in that court with the stars above, and now and then the green glare of the German flare freezing us all into statues, then the sudden spurt of his match, and the hiss of the rocket soaring up over the roofs. A few minutes later our own barrage came down about our own ears. The shells came perilously close. That morning they had caught some of our own men falling short, I was told. Under cover of the fire from our batteries the evacuation of the wounded went on.

CHAPTER XVIII

LAST HOURS IN FISMETTE

IN THAT great time there was never any rest or let-up until the body was killed, or it sank exhausted.

That night we set to work immediately to try to get Captain Williams of "A" company across the river before daylight. He had been struck by a machine gun bullet in the attack that morning. The bullet had travelled around his ribs and, lodging under the spine, had paralyzed him.

Last Hours in Fismette

He lay in another little dugout—a wine cave, too—about ten houses up the street from the big cave in the court. I made my way up to him through the houses and tried to cheer him by telling him we had come to get him. He was so cheerful and kindly and glad to see us, it would have brought the tears to our eyes—at any other time. Getting him out was not such an easy task.

It was impossible even to appear in the street. Lieutenant Glendenning lay dead there, shot through the heart, fine brave heart, I couldn't help crying when I heard of that—and we would have to knock holes through the walls of the houses to get Captain Williams' stretcher through from house to house.

We picked some strong Italians and started working through the big court, battering away with logs and picks, dislodging rocks from the mud plaster and working like mad in a race against time—for if it was morning before we reached the captain, he would have to stay another day in Fismette—and that might be fatal. We could use no lights. I can still see those dark figures battering away, then crawling through, choosing the space in the next wall for the tunneling, and going on and on. At last towards morning the passageway was ready and we carried the captain down as far as the court, lifting him through the holes in the wall with great care, sliding the stretcher from room to room, but it was too late. We had to stay in the big cave with Captain Haller's command post, where they brought a great many other wounded.

In there was a dressing station. One of the hospital corps worked night and day, poor lad! He was almost all in. The place had rows of wounded in it, moaning, and he had little with which to help them. Bandages were running out. In the cave there was a light, and hay on the floor. It ran far back into the hill. Some of us crawled in there and towards morning got some sleep. The last thing I heard was Captain Williams cheering some of the wounded, especially one Italian lad who was in great pain.

That night, and part of the next day, was fairly quiet. There was nothing to eat. Yes—something— one of my own men, who had heard that I had got back, brought me some fish, about half a cupful, and asked me to share it. He was so much in earnest about it, that I ate it with him like a sacrament.

Next morning not a shot could be heard, and it was warm and sunny. I got up and walked up the line of houses between the street and the hill, working from back yard to back yard. The little dugout where Captain Williams had been the night before, I determined to make my headquarters, and as a sign of authority carried my officer's raincoat there. There were one or two men sleeping in it and some wounded. Up above it on the hillside was a house which overlooked the fields beyond. There we had an observation post. A garret in one of the houses

Last Hours in Fismette

along the street sheltered one of our invaluable machine guns and its valiant crew. A few of our lads were still lying along the wall as sentries. The rest were down in the houses. The wall and the space in front of it for many yards had dead men lying every here and there.

Farther along near the cross street, I found some of our men in a house which had a spring in it. Here one of our wounded sergeants, Davidson, lay near the water. A fine chap and very glad to see me. He had heard I had been killed. We moved him down to the big cave and got him across the river later. Lieutenant Horner was holding this end of the line. The men were sitting around in the rooms of the little deserted houses, waiting for anything that might happen, and hoping that nothing would. Night was the time we all dreaded. The days seemed easy in comparison.

As we could not use the street, I felt the need of quick communication up and down the line and set some of the men to completing the knocking of holes between houses. In the barn by the court, I started, with Captain Haller's sanction, a number of men digging a tunnel under the narrow street so we could cross into the houses on the other side and occupy them also. Captain Thompson and I went up a few houses and tried to "fish" Lieutenant Glendenning's body from the street where it was lying face downward, by making a loop, getting it around him, and then dragging him in through the window, but we could not make it. It was impossible to show oneself even for a minute in the street and the rope we had was a miserable stiff piece of old hemp that forever slipped. We had to give it up. I went back to see how the tunnel was coming on.

The men were digging, standing in one room of the barn while some of us stood talking in the next, when, without any warning but a swift whistle, a trench mortar shell fell through the roof and exploded in the room where the men were working, killing and wounding about eight or nine. A lot of fragments came through the door into our room and one struck me on the knee. It seemed nothing at the time with so many killed. One or two of the poor

lads who had been digging were carried into the
cave, one fellow had his face blown full of dirt and
stones, and was frightfully shell shocked, jerking
and crying out pitifully.

There is certainly such a thing as shell shock, and
a very terrible thing it is, not to be explained away
by doctors who write articles for the library table
magazines. The rest of the poor, black, dust-covered
bodies were buried in the pit they had dug for themselves, or in the hole the shell had made. All those
dead faces were covered with an ashen-gray dust,
and there was a hellish scent of high explosive in the
air. That was about noon.

About three o'clock Major Donnely appeared
among us, having crossed the bridge, like the brave
man he was, in daylight. He had orders to make another attack. That is, his battalion was to attack
while what was left of ours was to hold the town.

It was a frightful order, murder. All of us knew
that. I tried to explain the situation to the major,
thinking he did not know that he was flinging three
companies against the German army, but I left off,
seeing that he did know and was only carrying out
what he had been ordered to do.*

The companies that had come into town the night

* The orders for this attack and for the whole Fismette fiasco, it now ap-
pears, had come from the French Army Commander through the 3rd Corps
headquarters. The tactical reason seems to have been that the Fismes-
Fismette bridgehead was worth all that it might cost. See Major General
Bullard's Memoirs and his letter to General Pershing of August 28, 1918.

before were to make the attack. I talked to Fletcher, who came up looking very grave and sad over it. I remember he looked at me significantly as the men filed out. Captain Thompson led. That was the last time I ever saw either him or Fletcher.

We of the first battalion left in Fismette got our men sheltered as well as we could for the barrage which we knew was sure to follow, and at the same time kept up a sharp watch. The other companies marched out of the town to the left and made an at-

tack up the hill. It was not hard to tell when the battle was on.

I took my station in the observation house above the little dugout. One of our scouts was there. "Look here, lieutenant," said he, and between the cracks in the roof pointed out a haystack about fifty yards away. I looked at it carefully through his glass. From it poked the ugly nose of a machine gun from which went up a faint blue haze. Oh! if we had only had rifle grenades then!

271

Toward the Flame

The whole hill seemed to be alive with machine guns and artillery. Such a barrage fell on Fismette that we were instantly driven from our posts into the dugout. In the yard beside us shell after shell smashed. We closed the iron door to our cave to keep out the fragments, but the choking gas and the smell of high explosives came in. Above all the roar suddenly sounded, seemingly right above our heads, the sharp bark of our own single machine gun. Brave lads, they were still sticking to it in the garret. We knew they had only one box of ammunition left. Houses along the street were blown up and disappeared inwardly in a cloud of dust and a sliding noise. I hopped out once to see Major Donnely at the big cave.

"Hang on," he said.

After what seemed an eternity, some one came and said our men were coming back—then our own barrage fell. It was the greatest we had thrown around there. The hillside was tossed about for an hour and the German shells had ceased. As always, when it lifted, there followed the silence of the dead. We were all breathing in relief when what was left of the other companies returned. It was a miserable remnant. The loss had been terrific. Some of the companies were down to a few men. The gain had been nothing and we had exposed the smallness of our force to the Germans. A German plane came down so close it seemed to glide along the roofs. All was silent in the courts and houses till it passed. The aviator could have counted our buttons. No one was fool enough to shoot at him. As usual at that time, the Germans owned the air.

Captain Thompson had been killed, hit by a shell, some of his men said, while he was shouting to them to rally for the third time. The survivors were all in no shape to stand any further strain, having borne all that flesh and blood could, and more. The town was choked with dead and wounded. Even my own little dugout was full of them by this time.

About nightfall the little lieutenant,* who had our third platoon on the left flank, came up to tell me there was nobody left there. He was badly wounded and half out of his head. The story of his platoon is an heroic one. All alone on the left flank, they held on and on, the little groups at the barricade and in the shell-holes gradually becoming less and less, till *no one* was left. My fine little Italian striker, Nick de Saza, had his head taken off by a shell, working his *Chauchat* automatic to the last. I sent the lieutenant over with some of the other wounded. They got back that night into Fismes. He was too young to die miserably of gas after being wounded.

That night—unforgettable—darkness settled down on a despairing but determined little group of survivors in Fismette. Every now and then one of our

* Lieutenant Francis Welton, I have since learned.

machine guns barked from the roof, and, as ever at dark, the German flares began. There were very few of us left to hold the line. We got instructions from the major about dusk, and some hope of relief, but I knew that it was only to hearten us. On the other side of the river no one knew what was going on. I tried to string my men out along the wall, but there were so few, I felt it was better to keep most in shelter and some sentries along the wall. We could at least rush out then and make a stand. The last of our remaining officers in "B" company, Lieutenant Gerald, came up and joined me with a remnant of men. He was all in, almost out of his head with fatigue and two days on the line without sleep or food, but still wonderfully game. The dugout filled up with wounded and gassed men, two layers deep. It was a crazy house in there.

I went up in the little house on the hill just above, where we had been observing. A shell fell in the garden, and by its red flash I saw a picture of Christ on the wall. The thorn-crowned face leaped suddenly out of the frame at each devil's candle. Simplehearted Catholic peasants had lived there once. I saw that picture by the same light a good many times that night. It was a real piece of melodrama.

We arranged a regular system of reliefs, the men taking turns on the line and then in the dugout. To crawl out onto that line among the dead men by the wall in the tense darkness, shells whistling and falling, and now and then a flare of a corpse-like light, was a terrific test for a man. It grew harder and harder to get the men to leave the dugout as the shelling kept up.

Towards morning the shelling stopped. I began to realize that all the men by the wall were dead. One young Italian whose turn it was to go on post whimpered and begged—he was sick, he said. God knows, we all were! I was numbly trying to think what I could do with him, when the barrage fell. All that were still outside made for the dugout. We crawled in over the wounded and sat shaking. I knew when it lifted that we must meet an attack.

In all that awful uproar I heard some one at the door. The men next to it did not want to open it. It took me some time to give orders to let him in. I was getting very hazy. The poor devil came in shaking and crying. It seemed as though the place was afire outside. We slammed the door again— "gas!" "gas!"—on went the masks. It was real this time. The wounded begged piteously to be helped into theirs and everybody did what they could. A shell-shocked man was shouting and jumping about. Some one held him down, cursing him. Then came the direct hit—a great stunning blow on the top of the dugout; everybody was quieted by that, and the smell of explosive was intense! Gradually I heard the faint stir in the darkness again and the voices through the gas masks. The cave had held. "Open

the door!" cried somebody, "and beat out the gas."
We did so and I saw that it was quiet again outside.

That meant only one thing. I felt—an attack—
but I seemed to know it without being able to do
anything about it. It was a long time seemingly be-

fore I moved myself with great effort. Then I tried to get the men up on the line again. We were all choking with gas. I heard Gerald pleading and remonstrating; he was trying to be very logical. "Don't you see?" I heard him say. "All right, I'll go then," and he started up in the darkness after a few of the others who had gone already to man the line. I stood trying to get the men out of the dugout, half wondering what I was trying to do at times and then remembering. It was strangely quiet.

Some one came and said, "They are all dead up there along the wall, lieutenant, and there's no one between us and 'C' company. The machine gun is knocked out." I tried to think this out.

Suddenly along the top of the hill there was a puff, a rolling cloud of smoke, and then a great burst of dirty, yellow flame. By its glare I could see Gerald standing halfway up the hill with his pistol drawn. It was the *Flammenwerfer,* the flame throwers; the men along the crest curled up like leaves to save themselves as the flame and smoke rolled clear over them. There was another flash between the houses. One of the men stood up, turning around outlined against the flame—"Oh! my God!" he cried. "Oh! God!"

Here ends this narrative.

ADDENDA

THE following extract, taken from a newspaper
clipping of *First War Memoirs of an A.E.F.
Commander,* by Major General R. L. Bullard, U. S.
A., gives a more "official" version of the fighting
about Fismes and Fismette with some interesting
side-lights on the affair from "higher up":

In Fismette, the portion of the village of Fismes
on the north side of the Vesle, I had a single company of infantry, 150 men of the 28th (Pennsylvania) Division. One day I was ordered to make
a raid with this company. It was made with great
determination, but the bluffs of the river to the east,
north and northwest were lined with enemy machine
guns, and the company, thus covered on three sides

278

by the enemy's fire, had no success. It was driven back into its cellars in Fismette.

This company could be reinforced and fed at night only across a broken bridge, now not even a footbridge. This crossing was swept from two directions by enemy machine-gun fire, and men crossed, whether by day or night, only at intervals, and then only a man at a time. In short, men could not cross. It was evident that whenever the enemy desired he could wipe out the company on the north bank of the Vesle.

After its failure in the raid, as ordered by our French general, I ordered that company withdrawn to the south bank of the Vesle River, man by man, at night. My chief-of-staff, who was very much in favor of the general's idea of bridge-heads, knew of the order which I was going to give. When I returned from Fismes late in the afternoon I found our French general at my corps headquarters, and that my chief-of-staff had informed him of my order to withdraw the company. The French army commander ordered me at once to replace it. It was done.

COMPANY IS WIPED OUT

Three or four days after this affair, without my ability to reinforce it or save it, completely at the mercy of the enemy, this company was wiped out by an enemy attack. Then I noticed that the French communiqué of the day reported that my 3rd Corps had repulsed an enemy attack. When the French army commander appeared at my corps headquarters he offered me as consolation for his error this French communiqué. It was at least acknowledgment of the responsibility for the mistake.

But it did not console me for the only accident of my military career. I reported it at once to the American Commander-in-Chief, General Pershing, in the following letter:

Headquarters 3rd Army Corps,
American Expeditionary Forces, France,
A.P.O. 754, August 28, 1918.

General J. W. McAndrew, G.H.Q., A.E.F.:
My Dear General:

I am informed that to-day's German communiqué (which I have not seen) states that the Germans captured at Fismette yesterday 250 Americans. A part of my command until yesterday occupied Fismette. I had there some 190 officers and men altogether infantry. If you will look upon the map you will see the position of Fismes, a large village on the south bank of the Vesle. Just opposite Fismes, on the north bank, is the small village of Fismette. Opposite Fismes the village of Fismette, and no more, was occupied by us. Ten days ago, after a German attack upon Fismette, which almost succeeded,* I saw

* This refers to the time and the events described in the last two chapters above.

that Fismette could not be held by us against any real attempt by the Germans to take it, and that to attempt to continue to hold it would, on account of the lay of the surrounding terrain, involve the sure sacrifice of its garrison, to which help could not be sent except by driblets at night. I therefore decided to withdraw the garrison of Fismette some 300 mètres back across the Vesle River into Fismes. Before this was finished the French general commanding the 6th Army, to which I belong, arrived at my headquarters, and, learning of my orders for withdrawal from Fismette, himself, in person, directed me to continue to hold Fismette and how to hold it. My orders were changed in his presence and his orders were obeyed. Yesterday morning, the Germans made a strong attack upon Fismette from two directions, taking the village and killing or capturing almost all of our men who were in it.

I request that the Commander-in-Chief be acquainted with the facts in this case.

R. L. BULLARD,
Major-General, N.A., Commanding 3rd Army Corps.

PERSHING IRRITATED

A few days later I saw General Pershing himself. He told me that he had seen the letter, that he understood. He was much irritated and asked me with vehemence:

"Why did you not disobey the order?"

I did not answer. It was not necessary to answer. The general had spoken in the vehemence of his irritation.

While I recall this incident with some bitterness, I must still give the French general credit for being ever ready to help and helping me and my corps. And he was a fighting man. He never ceased to press the enemy.

THE END

CPSIA information can be obtained
at www.ICGtesting.com
Printed in the USA
FFOW03n0648010815
15619FF

CPSIA information can be obtained
at www.ICGtesting.com
Printed in the USA
FFOW03n0648010815
15619FF

9 780803 259478